**JOHN WITTICH**
*Citizen and Woolman of London*

*Discovering*
# London Villages

SHIRE PUBLICATIONS LTD

# Contents

1. Battersea     3
2. Chelsea     7
3. Chiswick     12
4. Clapham     16
5. Fulham     19
6. Greenwich     24
7. Hammersmith     29
8. Hampstead     33
9. Highgate     38
10. Islington     45
11. Kew     48
12. Paddington     54
13. Stoke Newington     59
Index     64

ACKNOWLEDGEMENTS
The maps of Chelsea, Hammersmith, Islington and Stoke Newington are by Richard G. Holmes.
The cover design is by Ron Shaddock.

Printed in Great Britain by C. I. Thomas & Sons (Haverfordwest) Ltd, Press Buildings, Merlins Bridge, Haverfordwest, Dyfed.

# 1. Battersea

Mention Battersea to people today and they might well react 'Dogs' Home', 'Festival Gardens', or even 'Power Station'. Others may well have heard of the Battersea Shield, a fine piece of iron-age workmanship now in the British Museum, or of the Battersea (de Morgan) Pottery.

The name is shown as *Patricsey* Island in the Domesday Survey of 1086 and means Peter's Island, for Battersea was once owned by the monks of Westminster Abbey, whose patron saint was Saint Peter. After the Reformation and the Dissolution of the Monasteries in the sixteenth century the manor passed to the St John family and the Earls of Spencer. Prior to the developments of the late eighteenth and early nineteenth centuries the main occupation of the local inhabitants was market-gardening and one of the main products was simples (medicinal herbs), which were supplied to the apothecaries of London. The saying 'You must go to Battersea to get your simples cut' derives from this side of life in the former village. It is used as a reproof to a simpleton or somebody who has made a very foolish observation.

Today Battersea forms part of the London Borough of Wandsworth, under the London Government Act 1963, and although it has been absorbed into a large municipal authority's area it still retains much of its village atmosphere.

The origin of the **Battersea Dogs' Home** (1), in Battersea Park Road, was the desire of a Mrs Tealby to do something for the thousands of dogs who ran free in the streets of Victorian London, particularly in the Holloway area of north London. After early teething troubles — neighbours, finance and housing — the home settled in Battersea in 1871. Stray dogs from all over the Greater London Council's area are brought to the home, and a rate of some sixty a day has been recorded. Since its original opening in north London in 1860 over two million dogs have been taken in and looked after. A condition of buying a dog from the home — some two thousand are sold every year — is that it will not be used for experiments or for public entertainment.

Standing like a prehistoric monster with its feet pointing to the sky are four of the tallest chimneys in London, rising 300 feet into the air and belonging to the **Battersea Power Station** (2). The building was designed by Sir Giles Gilbert Scott (1880-1960) and erected between 1932 and 1934; the station supplies electricity for an area extending from Greenwich to Maidenhead and from Chertsey to Chesham. When the foundations were being dug, a 2,000-year-old skull was found in the riverbank. The absence of cooling towers is explained by the fact that the central heating for the Pimlico Estate, on the opposite bank of the river, is supplied by pipe from the station.

3

The station's next-door neighbour is a gasometer which also stands 300 feet high, measures 180 feet across and is capable of holding seven million cubic feet of gas. With the advent of North Sea gas this landmark will, in the future, disappear from London's skyline.

Across the road from the power station is one of London's loveliest open spaces, **Battersea Park** (3), which was the work of Sir James Pennethorne (1801-71), the stepson of John Nash, George IV's favourite architect. There are two 'sides' to the park; one is the Festival Gardens, established here as part of the Festival of Britain in 1951, and the other has acres of playing fields, an English garden, a cricket ground and a fine running track. In addition there are a boating lake, flowerbeds and winding paths to intrigue visitors. Before the park was laid out, the marshland was used by market-gardeners who, it is said, first grew asparagus here. Gentlemen fought duels here, amongst them the first Duke of Wellington (1769-1852) and the Earl of Winchelsea. The duel took place because Lord Winchelsea had accused the Duke of dishonesty in connection with the Catholic Emancipation Bill. Apparently it was the Duke's intention to fire his pistol at his opponent's legs - but he missed! Lord Winchelsea fired into the air, apologised to the Duke, and honour was satisfied - and all this at eight o'clock in the morning! At that time there were extensions being carried out to the London docks, and the earth removed from them was transported to fill in the marshland of Battersea Fields, as the area now occupied by the park was then known.

At either end of Battersea Park are suspension bridges over the Thames, the one to the east, **Chelsea Bridge,** dating from 1937 when it cost £85,000. It replaced a bridge built in 1858 and which, until 1897, was a toll-bridge. One of the few surviving nineteenth-century suspension bridges over the river is the **Albert Bridge** (4), which links the Chelsea Embankment, opened between 1871 and 1874, with Battersea on the south bank of the river. The bridge was opened in 1873, the work of R. M. Ordish, who also designed the roof of St Pancras station; its central span is 400 feet, although since 1973 it has been supported from underneath and its future is in doubt. It is a good example of its date.

The next bridge upstream is **Battersea Bridge** (5). Designed by Sir Joseph Bazalgette (1819-90), it replaces the wooden bridge built between 1771 and 1773, which has been immortalised in James McNeill Whistler's painting of it. The central arch, the highest of the set, allows the larger tankers and other vessels to pass through on their way up river.

The **Parish Church of Saint Mary the Virgin** (6) was rebuilt in 1777 by Jos. Dixon, who is described as being 'a builder of Westminster'. Here William Blake (1757-1827), artist, poet and mystic, married Katherine, the daughter of a market-gardener. Although unable to write her name, she 'signed' the marriage

## BATTERSEA

1 Battersea Dogs' Home
2 Battersea Power Station
3 Battersea Park
4 Albert Bridge
5 Battersea Bridge
6 Parish Church of Saint Mary the Virgin
7 Church Dock
8 Raven public house
9 Vicarage Crescent
10 Old Battersea House
11 Castle public house
12 Sir Walter St John School

register with a cross; she was a devoted wife and Blake could not resist painting her on his deathbed. The east window comprises the finest seventeenth-century stained glass, full of heraldic devices. Possibly the work of Bernard van Linge, one of the greatest glass-workers of his time, the window is said to have come from the previous church. It was given by St John St John and shows his relationship with the royal house of Tudor. Included are portraits of Margaret Beauchamp, Henry VII and Elizabeth I, with their coats of arms and those of the St John family. The windows either side of the main one are eighteenth-century and the work of James Pearson. The registers, an almost complete set from 1559, contain a number of interesting entries and signatures. William Wilberforce witnessed a wedding conducted by the Rev. John Venn, Rector of Clapham; both men were founder members of the Clapham Sect, a group determined to free all slaves in the British Empire, an aim they were successful in fulfilling in due course. There is also record of the burial of the American general

Benedict Arnold on 14th June 1801 and his wife, Margaret, on 25th August 1804. J. W. M. Turner, the artist (1775-1851), used to sit in the vestry at the west end of the church to paint the sunsets over the Thames. In spite of more recent building on the other side of the river, the sunsets can still be enjoyed today. In the crypt can be seen, mounted on the walls, sixty of the lead inscriptions from the three hundred coffins once buried here. On the inside walls of the church are many memorials and monuments all of which are worth reading. On the south wall of the gallery is Sir Edward Wynter's monument from the old church. It tells how he crushed to death a tiger and overthrew sixty Moors in single conflict. In the western section of the churchyard lies buried William Curtis, who died in 1799. He was an eminent botanist, whose great contribution to horticulturists and agriculturalists was his book on British grasses. He also produced an illustrated book on wild plants around London.

Just outside the west end of the churchyard is **Church Dock** (7), a local landing stage and hithe - a dock cut into the riverbank. It was here that in the old days local inhabitants would unload their goods from barges and lighters.

In the former village square, now Battersea Square, stands the **Raven** public house (8) with its seventeenth-century Dutch-style gables, a reminder that the square was a general meeting place hundreds of years ago. It is said that Charles II (1630-85) frequently used the ferry from Chelsea, where doubtless he had been to see the lovely Nell Gwynne and visited the Raven after bathing in the river. On one occasion Colonel Thomas Blood, who achieved notoriety in the seventeenth century by trying to steal the Crown Jewels from the Tower of London, lay in wait for the king. But at the last moment he could not bring himself to kill Charles and, on confessing his crime, received a royal pardon and a pension. The reason for the pension, the princely sum for those days of £500, has never been revealed.

Leading out of the square is **Vicarage Crescent** (9), where can be found Devonshire House and the old vicarage, both of which date from the eighteenth century, reminders of the numerous similar houses which once adorned the riverbank. On the wall of the old vicarage is a blue plaque recording that Edward Adrian Wilson, the famous Antarctic explorer and naturalist, lived in the house. Born at Cheltenham in 1872, he was one of the party of five who reached the South Pole on 12th January 1912. His body was found with those of Scott and Bowers after their ill-fated attempt to return to HMS *Discovery*, the base ship for the expedition.

Although now cut off from the river by a main road, the seventeenth-century **Old Battersea House** (10), said by some to have been designed by Sir Christopher Wren (1632-1723), has been leased to the Forbes Foundation of America. When in the 1930s the immediate area was being redeveloped by Battersea Borough Council, Colonel and Mrs Stirling bought a life tenancy of the building, and soon the house was attracting visitors by the score to see their collection of Pre-Raphaelite paintings by Evelyn de Morgan, Mrs Stirling's sister, and the ceramics of William de Morgan. In addition, the Stirlings had gathered together a fine collection of seventeenth-century furniture. It is hoped that the ground-floor rooms of the house may open as an art gallery and museum in memory of its late occupants and their works of art.

Further redevelopment in the area of Battersea High Street in recent years has meant the demolition of a number of the older houses which used to abound in this neighbourhood, including the sixteenth-century tavern, the **Castle** (11). However, the tavern has since been rebuilt and the original Tudor inn sign, carved from a solid piece of wood, can now be seen outside the new house.

For the first hundred and fifty years of its existence the **Sir Walter St John School** (12) was the only school in Battersea, having been founded by the third baronet in 1700 'for the education of twenty free scholars', but it has since been rebuilt and enlarged in 1859 and 1915. Over the archway into the school can be seen the arms and motto of the St John family - *Rather deathe than false of faythe.*

---

# 2. Chelsea

It is said that Chelsea was originally called *Celchyth,* meaning a hithe (landing place) for chalk or lime, but Norden, writing in the seventeenth century, claims that it was a strand or riverside roadway, like a chesil, 'which the sea casteth up', made of sand and pebbles from the river.

Connecting the north (Chelsea) and south (Battersea) banks of the river is **Chelsea Bridge** (1) (see page 4). From the bridge one has a fine view of the Chelsea skyline.

Leave the bridge and make your way to the **Chelsea Embankment** (2), constructed by Sir Joseph Bazalgette, the engineer, and completed in 1871. Built into the side of the embankment is a tunnel, the present-day outlet for one of London's lost rivers, the **Westbourne** (3). This is visible from the bridge.

On the site of a monastic almshouse and theological college Charles II founded in 1682, perhaps with the help of Nell Gwynne, the **Royal Hospital** (4) as a place of retirement for veteran soldiers from the recently established standing army of England. In the grounds of the Hospital the Chelsea Flower Show takes place each May. We shall visit the hospital again later on our tour of Chelsea.

Continue along the riverside to Chelsea's **Botanical Gardens** (5), founded in 1673 by the Society of Apothecaries of the City of

London. The freehold was given to the Society by Sir Hans Sloane on condition that the gardens were kept 'for the manifestation of the glory, power and wisdom of God'. The cotton seeds used for the first cotton fields in the United States were grown here. Today the establishment is devoted to research and visitors are not allowed into the gardens, though they may peep through the wrought iron entrance gates.

**Cheyne Walk** (6) has had many distinguished residents. The novelist George Eliot (the pen name of Mary Ann Cross, nee Evans) is commemorated by a blue plaque on No. 4, where she moved towards the end of her life. Her next-door neighbour at No. 5 was John Camden Nield, the musician, who bequeathed £500,000 to Queen Victoria. At No. 6 at the end of the eighteenth century an Italian doctor called Dominietti spent £37,000 in establishing a fashionable bathing centre for medicinal purposes. No. 10 was once the residence of Lloyd George and, later, of Archbishop Davidson, Archbishop of Canterbury from 1903 to 1928. Built in 1717, No. 16 was first occupied by Robert Chapman, whose monogram RC can be seen on the wrought-iron gateway, and later by Dante Gabriel Rossetti and Algernon Charles Swinburne. James McNeill Whistler, the American artist, lived for a time at No. 21. Henry VIII built a palace here but nothing of it remains above ground except a small hunting lodge in nearby Glebe Place.

**Cadogan Pier** (7) has been passed before we reach Rossetti's house but, looking back, both the pier and the **Albert Bridge** (8) can be seen. The annual Doggett's Coat and Badge rowing race takes place on the river here. The race was inaugurated to commemorate the accession of George I in 1714 and the establishment of the House of Hanover on the British throne. The Albert Bridge, built to the designs of R. C. Ordish and opened in 1873, is of cantilever and suspension construction. Its structure has become fragile over the past few years and there is concern about its future.

With the growth in the population of the parish in the late eighteenth and early nineteenth centuries a new church became necessary. A new site was found, in St Luke's Street, and the old parish church of **All Saints** (9) was demoted to become a daughter church to the new church. Extensive damage by Second World War bombs has been repaired and the building today is a fine example of a church of the medieval and later periods. Thomas More's chapel, built for him in 1528, is a very early example of the Renaissance influence.

Opposite the west tower of the church are the **Margaret Roper Gardens** (10), made since the war and a pleasant oasis for the weary walker to rest in. Margaret Roper was the daughter of Thomas More; she rescued her father's head, which had been

# CHELSEA

1 Chelsea Bridge
2 Chelsea Embankment
3 Outlet of Westbourne
4 Royal Hospital
5 Botanical Gardens
6 Cheyne Walk
7 Cadogan Pier
8 Albert Bridge
9 All Saints church
10 Margaret Roper Gardens
11 Site of house of Sir John Danvers
12 Crosby Hall
13 More's Garden
14 Battersea Bridge
15 Mrs Gaskell's house
16 Lindsay House

17 River boats
18 Moravian Cemetery
19 King's Road
20 Catholic chapel
21 Paultons Square
22 Henry VIII's hunting lodge
23 Carlyle's House
24 Church of the Holy Redeemer
25 Upper Cheyne Row
26 Oakley Street
27 Tite Street
28 White House
29 National Army Museum
30 Chelsea Barracks
31 Grosvenor Canal entrance (site of)

placed on top of the south gate of the City of London after his execution on Tower Hill in 1535. In 1969 Cubitt Bevis's statue of Thomas More was unveiled in front of the church.

Sir John Danvers, one of the signatories to the death warrant of Charles I, built himself a house here (11) in the seventeenth century, but nothing of it remains.

Moved to its present site in the early twentieth century, **Crosby Hall** (12) was once the home of the Crosby family. Originally built in 1466 in Bishopsgate in the City, it was dismantled because of a road widening scheme and re-erected here. At one time Thomas More owned the house in the City, and it is appropriate that it should now stand here so near to where he lived.

On the corner of the embankment and Beaufort Street there is a block of flats called **More's Garden** (13). Look carefully at the decoration of the entrance step to see its floral tribute to Thomas's garden.

The present **Battersea Bridge** (14) was built in 1890 (see page 4).

**No. 96 Cheyne Walk** (15) was the home of Mrs Gaskell, the

9

novelist, who was born here in 1810.

Most of the grand houses and palaces have long since disappeared from the Chelsea riverside but **Lindsay House** (16) survives. Built in 1674, it was originally a single three-storeyed house, but a hundred years later it was divided into three houses. Here, in the eighteenth century, came Count Zinzendorf, a great benefactor of the Moravian Church; the house became the English headquarters of the church. At No.98 lived the Brunels, civil engineers, in the nineteenth century.

Across the road from Lindsay House are moored **river boats** (17), in which people live and work, so keeping alive this portion of the river.

Retrace your steps a short way and turn left up Milman's Street; on the right will be seen Moravian Place, which leads to the **Moravian Cemetery** (18), where members of the church are buried. The plot of ground is laid out in four squares, one quarter being used for the burial of married men, another for single men, and the other two for married and unmarried women. A small flat stone marks each grave and this led to the tradition that Moravians are buried standing up, with only one person to each grave. Permission to visit the cemetery can usually be obtained from the Moravian Church.

At the end of the street turn right along the **King's Road** (19), once the private road of the king leading from Westminster to Hampton Court. Today the road is the high street of Chelsea and a centre of fashion. Beaufort Street is soon reached; walk down it towards the river and on the left-hand side you will see a large rood, or crucifix, on the outside wall of a **Catholic chapel** (20). This chapel is on the site of the house in which Thomas More lived. Down the side of the building you will see the wall of the garden of the house. Until a few years ago the house and chapel were the home of an order of Catholic nuns, but they have moved out of London and the buildings are now occupied by a seminary. A mosaic on the side wall shows the head of Thomas More.

Return to the King's Road and on the right-hand side is **Paultons Square** (21). A walk round will show the unified pattern of the houses, built in the early nineteenth century.

Returning once more to the King's Road and passing Old Church Street and Bramerton Street, turn right into Glebe Place. At the end is the old **hunting lodge** of Henry VIII's palace (22), now used as a day nursery. Follow the street round, first to the right and then to the left. It meets Upper Cheyne Row and Cheyne Row, and at No. 24 Cheyne Row is **Carlyle's House** (23), maintained by the National Trust. Here the great historian, Thomas Carlyle, lived for nearly fifty years. His clothes are in the wardrobe and his double-walled refuge from the noise of the town still exists.

At the Glebe Place end of Cheyne Row is the Catholic **church of the Holy Redeemer and St Thomas More** (24); More's coat of arms is over the main entrance. It is sad that the church door has had to be caged in to prevent vandalism.

Walk along **Upper Cheyne Row** (25) and notice the curious numbering of the houses — there is no No. 26. Was one of the occupants superstitious of double thirteen? There is a plaque to Leigh Hunt on No. 22 and the delightful end house bears the date 1767.

At the end of the Row is **Oakley Street** (26). While the buildings are not of great architectural merit, the street has a number of associations with famous people. At No. 54 lived Robert Falcon Scott, the Antarctic explorer.

Turn left after leaving Upper Cheyne Row and return to the King's Road; turn right and walk along to Flood Street, on the right. Walk down this until Cheyne Walk appears on the right and Royal Hospital Road on the left. Follow the latter and soon the wall of the Botanical Gardens will be reached; and for another peep into the grounds turn right down Swan Walk, then follow Dilke Street into **Tite Street** (27). The artist Whistler came here in the late nineteenth century. Godwin designed the **White House** (28) for him and was also responsible for the Tower House and the Studios in the same street. For eleven years Oscar Wilde lived at No. 34, opposite which once stood the Victoria Hospital for Children, into which was incorporated Gough House, the Chelsea home of Sir Richard Gough, who gave his name to Gough Square in the City of London.

Having explored Tite Street, return to Royal Hospital Road, turn right, and the **National Army Museum** (29) is on the right-hand side. It covers the history of the Army from the seventeenth century to the outbreak of the First World War in detail; the story is brought up to date by the Imperial War Museum in Lambeth Road, SE1.

'Old soldiers never die, they only fade away' — so the ever popular song tells us, and what better place for them to fade away in than at the Royal Hospital. Entrance to the buildings and grounds of the hospital is either by the Chelsea Gate, nearest to the National Army Museum, or by the London Gate at the further end of the road. It is well worth a visit, especially if you can persuade one of the pensioners to act as your guide. Do not forget to visit the tiny museum near the London Gate.

Leaving by either gate, turn right and soon you will find yourself at crossroads. Opposite are the **Chelsea Barracks** (30) of the modern army and you have a choice of going left to Sloane Square, ahead to Victoria, or right down towards the river and Chelsea Bridge again.

If you choose the last, pass the barracks on your right, and at the junction of the roads and the bridge you will find on your left the entrance to the former **Grosvenor Canal,** now used as a refuse collection point by the City of Westminster, and the pumping station for a waterworks (31).

# 3. Chiswick

Over the years many famous people have been attracted to live in this charming village setting alongside the river Thames. Artists and writers have come here to work and architects have added their contribution.

As in many other places the village life centres around the parish church, with the 'big house' not far away down the lane. There have been sufficient ways in and out to help transport people and goods from place to place. The eventual explosion of population came in the late eighteenth and early nineteenth centuries.

In tenth-century Anglo-Saxon charters the name is given as *Ceswican,* which means 'cheese farm', cheese presumably being a local product at that time.

In keeping with the fashion of the time William Hogarth (1697-1764) moved out of London to Chiswick about 1749 and bought a house - **Hogarth's House** (1) - where he continued to live until his death in 1764. His widow lived on at the house, attending services at the parish church, 'a stately figure in a bath chair'.

Hogarth came from Westmorland stock. It was his father, Richard Hogarth, who left the North and came, with his family, to live in London. Originally William was bound by his father as an apprentice to a silversmith, but William had other ideas and at the end of his apprenticeship attended the School of Art run by Sir James Thornhill, the famous painter. At the age of twenty-two he set up in business on his own, but most of his early work appears to have been engravings for bills and tradesmen's shop-window cards, samples of which still exist today. In 1729 he married Jane Thornhill, having eloped with her to Paddington Green church; the marriage was against the wishes of her father, but the men were later reconciled.

Today his house is a museum, open to the public for a small fee, and examples of his work are on display, but to see his finest series of paintings -*The rake's progress* and *The election* - a visit to the Soane Museum at No. 13 Lincoln's Inn Fields should be made.

Opposite a modern industrial factory and alongside a very busy road, and yet holding its own against all these difficulties, stand **Boston House and Square** (2). Built in the late seventeenth century, the square forms a forecourt to the house and has been likened to the Albany in Piccadilly.

## CHISWICK

1 Hogarth's House
2 Boston House and Square
3 Page's House Cottages
4 Figurehead
5 Chiswick Eyot
6 Hogarth's tomb
7 Church of Saint Nicholas

8 Cenotaph of Ugo Foscolo
9 Whistler's tomb
10 Greenhouse in Italian Garden
11 Inigo Jones Gateway
12 Royal gardens
13 Chiswick House
14 Chiswick House grounds

Off Church Street is a private lane in which stand **Page's House Cottages** (3), undisturbed by the passing of time as they have been for three hundred years.

In Church Street, opposite a building of the late medieval period which was once known as the Burlington Arms, is a **figurehead** (4) from some ancient ship, together with an anchor and ship's wheel.

Peculiar to London's river are its 'eyots' - small islands - of which some are inhabited but others are resting places only for birds. **Chiswick Eyot** (5) has no regular residents but at low tide is often a source of great delight to little boys and girls, who wade out to the island, perhaps imagining themselves modern-day Robinson Crusoes.

When William Hogarth died in 1764 at his house in Leicester Square, he was buried in the churchyard of Saint Nicholas's, the parish church of Chiswick. **Hogarth's tomb** (6), restored by a descendant, bears the following epitaph:

13

Farewell, great painter of mankind
Who reached the noblest point of art
Whose pictured morals charm the mind
And through the eye correct the heart.

If genius fire thee, Reader, stay
If nature touch thee, drop a tear
If neither move thee, move away
For Hogarth's honoured dust lies here.

Serving as the parish church of Chiswick as it and its predecessors have done for centuries is the **Church of Saint Nicholas** (7). All that remains of the fifteenth-century and later church is the tower, the rest having being pulled down and rebuilt, in the Gothic style of architecture, by John Loughborough Pearson (1817-97) in 1882-4. It is said that within the area covered by the previous church two daughters of Oliver Cromwell were buried anonymously for fear of reprisals. Cromwell's daughter Mary married the Earl of Falconberg, whose country house, Sutton Court, was in Chiswick.

To the west of the church, in what has become Chiswick Cemetery, an extension to the former graveyard of the church, can be seen the **cenotaph** (empty tomb) of the Italian patriot and poet Ugo Foscolo (1778-1827) (8). When he died Garibaldi came and laid a wreath on his tomb. After the unification of Italy, in 1871, the body was exhumed and re-interred, with all the suitable honours, in Santa Croce, Florence. Today there is another inscription on the side of the former tomb, which reads: 'This spot, where for forty-four years the relics of Ugo Foscolo reposed in honoured custody, will be forever held in grateful remembrance by the Italian nations'.

Some 150 yards into the cemetery and lying alongside the wall is **Whistler's tomb** (9). James McNeill Whistler, born in 1834 at Lowell, Massachusetts, spent his later years in England, dying in London in 1903.

The name of Joseph Paxton (1801-65) is always associated with glasshouses and greenhouses; many English stately homes have conservatories designed by him. Here, within the grounds of Chiswick House, he designed the present **greenhouse** (10), having been associated with Chiswick from his younger days as a gardener.

Although designed in the first place by Inigo Jones (1573-1652) to be the watergate for Beaufort House in Chelsea, the **Inigo Jones Gateway** (11) seems to have settled in very well in its present situation. Pope wrote:

I was brought from Chelsea last year
Batter'd with wind and weather
Inigo Jones put me together

Sir Hans Sloan let me alone
Burlington brought me hither.

It was first erected at Chelsea in 1621 for the Duke of Beaufort.

King Edward VII (1841-1910) used to come to Chiswick House with his family during his holidays. The royal children, including the later King George V, were each allocated a small plot of land to look after. Today the park-keepers maintain these **royal gardens** (12).

Although earlier in its history a number of famous names are associated with **Chiswick House** (13), it was not until Richard Boyle (1695-1753), a great patron of the arts, succeeded to the title of Earl of Burlington that the villa of today comes into the story. After his first grand tour of Europe in 1714-15 he commissioned alterations to Burlington House in Piccadilly. However, during his visit to Italy in 1719 he acquired a fuller knowledge of architecture and in particular of the buildings of Andrea Palladio (1518-80), whose works were already known in this country through Inigo Jones, the scenic designer turned architect. Palladio's Villa Capra inspired Burlington to have built, attached to the Jacobean house here, a 'Temple of the Arts' in which he could keep his collection of books, manuscripts, and *objets d'art*. The villa, begun in 1725 and completed in 1729, was enlarged by James Wyatt (1746-1813), when he demolished the original house. In 1928 the whole estate came up for sale and but for the intervention of the local and county councils would today be a vast housing estate. In the period just after the Second World War the Ministry of Works and Public Buildings (now the Department of the Environment) took over the care of the villa. In their careful restoration of the villa they removed the additions of Wyatt and now the building presents itself to visitors as it was when it was first built in the early eighteenth century.

If the villa's design is the work of Lord Burlington, inspired by Palladio, then most certainly the laying out of the **grounds** (14) is that of William Kent (1684-1748). It was one of the earliest gardens to break away from the formal designs of the age of Wren and to produce an 'English garden'. Using the villa as an axis, the avenues and vistas present an example of the care and attention paid to landscaping in the eighteenth century. The cedars of Lebanon were planted, as saplings, in 1642, while the Classical bridge over the river, or canal, is the remaining work of James Wyatt. At various vantage points in the grounds obelisks are set up. One of these has incorporated in it a Roman tomb commemorating a husband, wife and child of the second century and coming from the Arundel Collection of marbles; another is in a pond in the amphitheatre. There are also an Ionic temple, a Doric column and the foundations of an orangery to be found within the gardens.

# 4. Clapham

Clapham, mentioned in the Domesday Survey of 1086 as *Clopeham* - 'ham' meaning homestead, and Clope or Cloppa being the family name of the Saxon inhabitants - is also taken to be 'the homestead on the hill'. The first mention of a church here is in the twelfth century; it was near to the site of the present Saint Paul's Church, Rectory Grove. Today Clapham is a thriving inner suburb of Greater London and can no longer be described as 'a village four miles from the City'. Few places more thoroughly repay the time spent on research into their past than Clapham does with its long and useful history. Through here have passed kings and queens of England on their way from one royal palace to another; here men and women of the arts have retired, perhaps for health reasons, and spent their last days walking across Clapham Common and enjoying the peace and quiet of earlier times.

Clapham Common today covers an area of 205 acres and there are four ponds for water enthusiasts to enjoy. The **Eagle Pond** (1), now used by fishermen and birds, gets its name from the eagles on a house, which has long since disappeared, in nearby Narbonne Avenue. On the **Long Pond** (3) model boatmen can try their skills against the wind and weather. It was originally called the Boathouse Pond because the lord of the manor maintained a boathouse here. The **Children's Lido Pond** (7), near the parish church, was once known as the Cock Pond, after the tavern opposite. It is also shown on maps as the Pound or Pit Pond because it came into being as a result of quarrying in the late eighteenth century for soil and gravel to raise the site of the new parish church.

On the south side of the common is a small oasis of houses and the **Windmill** public house (2). The inn sign today shows a picture of the post mill which may well be the one referred to in seventeenth-century documents and from which the inn gets its name. The Windmill dates from the eighteenth century and was the recognised starting point for local horse races over the common. Reference to the parish register of the early eighteenth century has brought to light the fact that the vestry meetings were held at the Cock, the Plough and the Windmill inns.

The **milestone** (4) on Clapham Common South Side, near the junction with Rookery Road, reads: Royal Exchange 4½ miles (on the east and west faces); Whitehall 4 miles (on the south). The north side is defaced.

The Catholic church of Clapham is **Saint Mary's** (5), which was built in 1851. When it was decided in the 1930s to build a new parish hall, the site in St Alphonsus Road was chosen. In digging for the foundations remains were found of a plague or pest hospice on the site. It was not uncommon in times of great

# CLAPHAM

1 Eagle Pond
2 Windmill public house
3 Long Pond
4 Milestone
5 Saint Mary's Catholic church
6 Lord Macaulay's house
7 Children's Lido Pond
8 Old fire station
9 John Bentley's house
10 Vicarage of Saint Peter's
11 Cromwell Lodge
12 Saint Paul's church
13 Turret Grove
14 Coade-stone doorway
15 Parish School
16 Roman altarstone
17 Holy Trinity Church
18 Church Buildings
19 Sir Charles Barry's house
20 Site of Pepys's house

pestilence for small 'villages' to be created outside established towns, away from the general population of the area. This was one of them.

The nineteenth-century historian and man of letters, Thomas, Lord Macaulay (1800-59), lived at **No. 5 The Pavement** (6), as did his father Zachary Macaulay, the philanthropist and campaigner for the abolition of the slave trade. A stone plaque today marks the house, which was described by Thomas as being 'a roomy, comfortable dwelling, with a small garden behind'.

Near to the area of the Old Town known as the Polygon is the nineteenth-century **fire station** (8). Its modern counterpart can be seen further round in Old Town, Clapham, close to No. 23 Old Town (10).

The architect of Westminster Cathedral, John Bentley, lived at **43 Old Town** (9), the end house of a charming row dating from the time of Queen Anne. A blue commemorative plaque now distinguishes this house from others in the terrace. Bentley came to live here in 1894, the year work started on the cathedral, and died here on 2nd March 1902. He is buried at Mortlake Cemetery.

At **23 Old Town** (10) can be seen an eighteenth-century house, the vicarage of Saint Peter's Church, Clapham Manor Street, with its original wrought iron railings. Had it not been for the persistence of a former vicar, the Rev. A. J. W. Pritchard, these valuable railings would have ended up during the Second World War as scrap iron. Returning home one day, with a preservation

17

order in his pocket, Mr Pritchard found workmen already removing the railings. On production of the necessary documents work ceased and the railings were stored safely in the vicarage until the end of the war.

**Cromwell Lodge** (11) is the name given to the house in Rectory Grove almost opposite Saint Paul's Church, because, it is said, Oliver Cromwell used it as a hideaway.

When the new church was built on the common, **Saint Paul's** (12), the original parish church, was allowed to fall into disrepair. However, with the growth of the area in the early nineteenth century, it was rebuilt and a number of the treasures from the earlier church were restored. 'A diligent, faithful and esteemed servant of Charles II and James II' is an apt description of William Hewer, whose memorial can be seen in the church. He was the great friend and partner of Samuel Pepys and it was to Hewer's house at Clapham that Pepys retired in 1700 and where he died in 1703. A monumental brass here reads: 'Here lies William Tableer, who died 13th October AD 1401, to whose soul may God be merciful, Amen'. Other monuments, including the Clerke (1589) and the Atkins of the seventeenth century, are worth noting. Although this church is often locked, a friendly approach to the vicarage at the entrance to the churchyard will bring the desired results.

**Turret Grove** (13), near which the manor-house once stood, is a reminder of the great Elizabethan mansion, which has long since disappeared, except, it is said, for the foundation of the turret that gives the street its name.

The entrance doorway of **No. 52 Rectory Grove** (14) is made of Coade stone and is very reminiscent of Portland Place in Marylebone.

The local **Parish School** (15) was founded here in 1648 but has outgrown the site and been rebuilt in Victoria Rise, off the North Side, Clapham Common.

In the forecourt of the local branch library is a **Roman altarstone** (16). Found in the grounds of Cavendish House at the turn of the century, it was presented to the library by Councillor Golds and is believed to date from the first century.

On the south-west corner of the **Holy Trinity Church** (17), 'the church on the common', can be found the war-scarred memorial stone to the Clapham Sect. This was a group of gentlemen from the parish who led the fight, and won, against slavery in the British Empire, who 'laboured so abundantly for national righteousness and the conversion of the heathen and rested not until the curse of slavery was swept away from all parts of the British Dominions'. The inscription goes on to list Charles Grant, Zachary Macaulay, Granville Sharp, John Shore, James Stephens, Henry and John Thornton, Henry and John Venn, and William Wilberforce. The memorial was unveiled in 1919.

Opposite the west end of Holy Trinity Church are the **Church Buildings** (18), which are said to have been designed by Sir Christopher Wren between 1713 and 1720. Captain Cook, eighteenth-century explorer of Australia and New Zealand, lived in Clarence House while the house to the left is supposed to be Clapham Academy, where Thomas Hood went to school and about which he wrote an 'Ode on a Distant Prospect of Clapham Academy', with its painful memories.

Sir Charles Barry, architect of the Houses of Parliament, lived from 1850 to 1860 in a house on North Side, Clapham Common (19). Today it is the **Hostel of God for the Sick and Dying,** run by the Anglican Order of Saint Margaret, whose mother house is at East Grinstead, West Sussex. It stands on ground that was once part of the gardens of the house in which Samuel Pepys died.

The seventeenth-century diarist Samuel Pepys lived at **The Great House** (20), for the last years of his life. Here he died in 1703 and was buried in Saint Olave's Church, Hart Street, in the City of London. John Evelyn, another diarist of the period, records how he visited Pepys at Clapham and found the house to be useful and capacious.

---

# 5. Fulham

The earliest mention of the village of Fulham is in a grant of the manor to Erkenwald, Bishop of London from 675 to 693, from Tyrhtilus, Bishop of Hereford 688-710, about the year 691, and it is then called *Fulanham.* In his book *Britannia,* the antiquarian writer William Camden (1551-1623) calls it Fulham - *Volucrum Domus* - where the birds live, or a place (home) of fowls. Other dictionaries translating the Saxon word describe it as meaning 'Foulham', because of the alleged dirtiness of the place, or as coming from the Anglo-Saxon legal word *ful,* meaning a burial place for criminals, in which case the *ham,* homestead, must have been added later.

Overlooking the river at the north end of Putney Bridge stands the parish church of Fulham, **All Saints** (1), with its fifteenth-century tower built of Kentish ragstone, the only surviving part of the church which stood here during the Middle Ages. The rest of the church was pulled down and rebuilt to the designs of Arthur Blomfield (1829-99) in the 1880s. The date of the consecration was 9th July 1881, and the reredos was added to the high altar by Heaton Butler and Bayne in 1885. There are a number of items from the previous church, including the font, which dates from 1622, and some of the monuments. One of these to Dorothy Clarke, who died in 1695, is the work of Grinling Gibbons (1648-

1721). Parts of the organ case are made up of the late seventeenth-century pulpit.

The church being close to Fulham Palace, the former home of the Bishops of London, it is hardly surprising that there are a number of their tombs in the churchyard. One, to Bishop Thomas Sherlock (1678-1761), under the east window of the church, is signed by John Vardy. Also in the churchyard is the grave of Mr and Mrs Murr; the latter died on 29th November 1820 and her epitaph reads:

To the memory of Isabella Murr.
Ye who possess the brightest charms of life,
A tender friend, a kind indulgent wife,
Oh learn their worth! In her beneath this stone
These pleasant attributes shone.
Was not true happiness with them combined?
Ask the spoiled being she's left behind.

After the death of her husband was added:
He's gone too.

Adjacent to the churchyard, on the north side, are **Sir William Powell's almshouses** (2) for twelve poor widows. Founded in nearby Back Lane in 1680, the former premises were sold, by auction, in 1870, when the present buildings were built. Architecturally they are Neo-Gothic in style and match in well with the design of the parish church. Notice the inscription 'God's providence, our inheritance' on the Church Gate end of the building.

Founded between 1672 and 1673, the **Fulham Potteries** (3) owe their existence to John Dwight of Oxfordshire about whose earlier life little is known save the fact that he served the Bishops of Chester between 1661 and 1671. In the latter year he patented his experiments with clay and other mineral substances (patent no. 164 of 1671), and moved to Fulham from Wigan - at that time a favourite palace of the Bishops of Chester - and set up his pottery here. A number of interesting items, the work of John Dwight, are now in the Victoria and Albert Museum, South Kensington, including a beautiful half-length figure of a lifeless female child - Lydia Dwight, his daughter, who died in 1673 aged six. John Dwight was born about 1640, died in 1703 and was buried in Fulham churchyard. John Doulton, who founded the Lambeth Pottery, served his apprenticeship here.

A contrast to the old parish church, **Saint Etheldreda's Church,** Fulham Palace Road (4), was rebuilt in 1958, following the bombing in the Second World War of the Victorian church. It is smaller than its predecessor and was designed by Guy Briscoe. The larger-than-life crucifix over the altar, carved by Rita Lang, is made of wood from Brighton Pier. The font is made out of copper

## FULHAM

1 All Saints Church
2 Sir William Powell's almshouses
3 Fulham Potteries
4 Saint Etheldreda's Church
5 Craven Cottage
6 Bishop's Park
7 Fulham Palace
8 Starting point of Oxford and Cambridge boat race
9 Putney Bridge
10 Saint Mary's Church, Putney
11 Hurlingham House and grounds
12 Broomhouse Dock

and the baptistery window, designed by Cater Shopland, shows Christ in glory in the centre, with the side lights showing the Sacraments in their biblical context and their modern counterparts.

**Craven Cottage** (5) was considered the prettiest specimen of cottage architecture in the early years of the nineteenth century. Built originally by the Margravine of Anspach when she was Countess of Craven, the interior offered its visitors architecture 'out of this world', with a Gothic dining room of very considerable dimensions. Sir Edward Bulwer-Lytton (1803-73), the novelist and statesman, lived here for a time and here wrote three of his novels, including *The last of the barons*. Today the Fulham Football Club's ground is on the site where the cottage stood, but the ground perpetuates the name.

21

Originally **Bishop's Park** (6) was part of the private grounds surrounding Fulham Palace, which as early as the sixteenth century had become famous for their beauty and the culture of rare and exotic plants and trees. Elizabeth I was pleased to receive from Edmund Grindal, Bishop of London 1559-70, gifts of fruit picked in these gardens. Later, in the seventeenth century, Henry Compton, Bishop 1675-1707, found great solace here during his banishment from London by James II. Doubtless, his talents and inspirations were conveyed to Mary II and Anne to whom he had been tutor, for both of these queens were enthusiastic gardeners. John Evelyn, the diarist and himself a great authority on trees, used to visit the gardens. On 11th October 1681 Evelyn wrote: 'I went to Fulham to visit the Bishop of London whose garden is exceeding beautiful'. Today the gardens form part of a very pleasant riverside public park.

Almost within the shadow of the parish church's tower stands **Fulham Palace** (7), the former palace of the Bishops of London. After the grant of the manor of Fulham to the Bishop of London in c 691 the manor-house became the country residence of the Bishops. For nearly thirteen hundred years it remained their palace, until in 1972 it was sold to the local council and a house in Westminster became London House. The moat, filled in in 1921, was nearly one mile in length and is said to have been built by a Danish army which once camped at Fulham. During the seventeenth century a sluice was constructed in order to cleanse the moat from time to time by allowing access to the tidal river Thames. Nothing remains above ground today of the original house, the oldest portion being the sixteenth-century courtyard built in the time of Richard Fitzjames, Bishop 1506-22, and a typical example of Tudor architecture. Two famous bishops of the English Reformation are closely associated with the hall. Bishop Edmund Bonner tried heretics here in the sixteenth century; it is said that the Pope wished to throw him into a cauldron of molten lead. Bishop Nicholas Ridley was himself burnt as a heretic in 1555. On the north side of the courtyard is Bishop Bonner's bedroom, said to be haunted by his ghost. In the nineteenth century the hall was converted into a chapel but in 1867 the Victorian architect William Butterfield (1814-1900) built the present chapel. The east window was installed as a memorial to Bishop William Wand's son, who was killed in a climbing accident in the Alps in 1934.

Every year the eyes of the public, particularly the rowing world, are focused on two stake-boats in the river near Putney Bridge, for this is the **starting point of the Oxford and Cambridge boat race** (8). The first race was rowed in 1829 over a course at Henley-on-Thames, Oxfordshire, but it was transferred in 1845 to its present course of four and a quarter miles from Putney to Mortlake.

Before 1729, when the first Fulham bridge was erected linking Putney, on the south (Surrey) side of the river, with Fulham, on the north (Middlesex) side, the Bishops of London owned the ferry which plied between the two banks of the river. In 1671 the first attempt was made to erect a bridge from Fulham to Putney, but the necessary parliamentary bill was defeated by sixty-seven votes to fifty-four. Eventually, however, parliamentary approval was gained, and the story of the bill's passage through Parliament has been preserved for us in Anchitelle Grey's *Debates of the House of Commons*, published in 1769. In consequence of the destruction of the ferry, the Bishops, their families and dependants were allowed to use the bridge free of toll. The password used was 'Bishop', and it was not unusual to hear bricklayers, carpenters and others call out the word when going to the Bishop's palace on their lawful duty.

**Putney Bridge** (9) replaced the old Fulham Bridge of 1729 and was opened in 1884. The noted civil engineer Joseph Bazalgette designed the present bridge, which took four years to build and cost £23,975.

From the time of William the Conqueror (1027-87) until the time of the Reformation in the sixteenth century the manor of Putney was held by the Archbishops of Canterbury and had a chapel of ease to Wimbledon. Rebuilt in the fifteenth century, **Saint Mary's Church, Putney** (10), was demolished, except for the tower and the Bishop West Chapel, in the early nineteenth century. Several monuments from the old church were transferred to the new building. At this time the Bishop West Chapel (West was Bishop of Ely from 1515 to 1534) was left intact and is a good example of a late Gothic fan-vaulted building. In 1973 the entire interior of the church was gutted by fire, but plans have been made to restore the church in consideration of the needs of the present-day parish. During the Civil War of the seventeenth century Generals Fairfax, Fleetwood, Ireton and Rich held a council of War sitting round the communion table of the church - wearing their hats!

Although today polo is no longer played at **Hurlingham** (11), the name continues to be associated with the sport by its followers. The Prince and Princess of Wales, later King Edward VII and Queen Alexandra, daughter of King Christian IX of Denmark, together with the Duke and Duchess of Edinburgh, were among the spectators at the first polo match played here, in 1874.

In 1760 the Bishop of London, Thomas Sherlock, gave permission to William Cadogan, a physician 'well-known in his profession', to build himself a new house in nine acres of land. The centrepiece of the present Hurlingham House was Dr Cadogan's 'cottage'; the rest of the building was added in the late eighteenth century by John Ellis.

According to tradition, Charles I (1600-49) used the ferry across the Thames from **Broomhouse Dock** (12) to the Feathers at Wandsworth. If the story is true, then he risked his life in doing so, for there are several recorded incidents of persons being found drowned, washed up in the dock. Broomhouse itself, described as being a little village by the riverbank in 1705, derives its name from the Anglo-Saxon word *brom*, meaning 'broom' or 'furze', the English bramble, which grew here abundantly at one time.

---

# 6. Greenwich

To arrive at Greenwich by river is to arrive in the time-honoured way, as thousands of nobles and lords, with their ladies, have done in times long past. It requires a little imagination today to dream away the deserted docks and the tall blocks of flats and to think of the pleasant countryside between the two historical places, London and Greenwich, which are now both well and truly part of the Greater London scene.

After a forty-five minute trip from Westminster Pier to Greenwich, a journey that passes many interesting sights of London, the boat ties up at Greenwich Pier, near the *Cutty Sark,* the late Sir Francis Chichester's *Gipsy Moth IV* and the Royal Naval College. A short walk from the pier brings one to the parish church of Greenwich, Saint Alphege's, but first a word about Greenwich itself.

Greenwich, a medieval fishing village whose name meant 'green village' to the Saxon and later settlers, owes its rise to fame from the development of its castle area into a palace 'fit for a king and his children'. Built for himself by Humphrey, Duke of Gloucester, by the riverbank, it was called 'Placenta' or 'Bella (beautiful) Court'. It was during the time of the Tudors that it became one of the favourite palaces of the royal family. Henry VIII (1491-1547), Elizabeth I (1533-1603) and her step-sister Mary I (1516-58) were all born here. Having established the shipyards at Deptford and Woolwich, Henry VIII was well able to keep an eye on their progress while out hunting and hawking in Greenwich Park. Armour made at Greenwich was the finest in Europe; there are a number of examples of it in the armouries of the Tower of London.

A raiding party of Danes, in 1012, captured and killed the twenty-eighth Archbishop of Canterbury on the site where now stands the parish church of Greenwich, **Saint Alphege's** (1). The present building, designed by Nicholas Hawksmoor (1661-1736), was built as a result of the collapse of the previous church's roof, after the parishioners had petitioned Parliament. A committee was set up to consider the application and, at the same time, the

## GREENWICH

1 Saint Alphege's Church
2 *Gipsy Moth IV*
3 Greenwich foot tunnel
4 *Cutty Sark*
5 Royal Naval College
6 Queen's House
7 National Maritime Museum

8 Greenwich Park
9 Statue of General Wolfe
10 Flamstead House and Royal Observatory
11 Vanbrugh's Castle
12 Trafalgar Tavern
13 Yacht public house
14 Trinity Hospital

situation in regard to other churches in London, Westminster and the suburbs. The result was the passing of the Fifty New Churches Act of 1711, which enabled Greenwich church to be the first of the new churches to be completed.

After the damage of the Second World War, the interior was redesigned by Sir Albert Richardson RA, but the carving by Grinling Gibbons (1648-1721) and the altar rails by Jean Tijou are original. There is also a keyboard dating from Tudor times on which Thomas Tallis (*c* 1505-85), 'father of English church music', is said to have played, and here too is the tomb of General James Wolfe, who was born at Westerham in Kent in 1727, died in 1759 at the Battle of Quebec, Canada, and was buried here.

The late Sir Francis Chichester sailed single-handed around the world in 1967 in **Gipsy Moth IV** (2), named after the aircraft he had flown, and on his return he was knighted by Her Majesty the Queen, using the sword with which Queen Elizabeth I had knighted Sir Francis Drake, in front of the Royal Naval College.

Walkers wishing to cross the river can do so simply by going under it, using the **Greenwich foot tunnel** (3). Built in 1902, it is 406 yards in length, and its northern exit, on the Isle of Dogs, brings one close to the **Waterman's Arms.** Formerly known as the Newcastle Arms, this houses a museum of Victoriana, ranging

25

from stuffed animals to prints of the music hall. The **Island Gardens** were opened in 1895 and commemorate the place Wren considered to have the best view across the river to Greenwich Palace.

Appropriate to its long connections with the sea, Greenwich was chosen to be the resting place of the last and perhaps the most famous of the old clippers, the **Cutty Sark** (4). She was launched at Dumbarton on the Clyde and registered in London by Captain John Willis, who was familiarly known as 'Old White Hat'. The name *Cutty Sark* was taken from the poem by Robert Burns, 'Tam O'Shanter', in which the witch nannie is described as being lapped and flanged in a cutty sark (a short chemise). The ship was officially opened by Her Majesty the Queen on 25th June 1957 and exhibits between decks the story of the *Cutty Sark,* as well as the Long John Silver collection of ships' figureheads.

During the reign of William III (1650-1702) and Mary II (1662-94) it was decided to found a hospital for seamen similar to the Royal Hospital for retired soldiers at Chelsea. The site of the King's House was chosen, although at first it was intended to leave this undisturbed, and Christopher Wren (1632-1723) was chosen as architect. Wren was responsible for the general layout of the buildings, but other architects, notably Nicholas Hawksmoor (1661-1736) and Sir John Vanbrugh were deeply involved in its construction. Since 1873 the buildings have been used as the **Royal Naval College** (5), a university for serving naval officers, providing them with specialised higher educational training. The principal buildings open to the public include the Painted Hall, the dining hall of the college. The walls and ceiling were painted by Sir James Thornhill (1675-1734) and took him twenty years to complete. He was paid at the rate of £3 per yard for the ceiling and £1 per yard for the walls, with a total bill of £41,000. The ceiling of the lower hall depicts the victory of William and Mary over tyranny and the triumph of the Glorious Revolution. A recent count revealed that there are 1,773½ bare bosoms on display! The upper hall ceiling shows the Golden Age of Peace and Prosperity under Queen Anne and her husband, Prince George of Denmark.

Across the courtyard from the hall is the chapel of the college; originally designed by Wren, it was rebuilt by James Stuart (1713-88) after a disastrous fire in 1779. The interior design is Neo-Grecian and the painting over the east end is by Benjamin West (1738-1820), the American artist, and shows the Preservation of Saint Paul after his shipwreck on Malta. The quoted fee for the work was £1,200, and the cost of the frame by Richard Lawrence was 50 shillings a foot.

The **Queen's House** (6) was originally designed by Inigo Jones in 1616 for Anne of Denmark (1574-1619), the wife of James I. It was not completed until 1635, when Queen Henrietta Maria (1609-69), wife of Charles I, lived in it. At this time the house spanned a main road and from the side gave the impression of being a triumphal arch. Today it is linked by an open colonnade to the National Maritime Museum, of which it forms an integral part. Built in the Palladian style, following the designs of Andrea Palladio (1518-80), the Italian architect, it was the first house in England to break away from the Tudor style of architecture. True to the tradition of royal houses, the Queen's House is said to be haunted.

Under an Act of Parliament of 1934 the **National Maritime Museum** (7) was set up to illustrate the maritime history of Great Britain; it was formally opened by George VI on 27th April 1937. It is hard to realise that this important national museum was so late arriving on the educational scene. The contents of the museum show the development of Great Britain as a seafaring nation; the special exhibitions mounted from time to time show the great extent of its scope. One of its greatest treasures is the uniform worn by Lord Nelson at the Battle of Trafalgar. It also has in its possession the last royal barge, belonging to William and Mary.

In the reign of Henry VI (born 1421, died 1471), Duke Humphrey fenced in some two hundred acres of what is now **Greenwich Park** (8) and stocked it with deer for royal hunting. Evidence of earlier occupation of the area has been found in the prehistoric tumuli and the remains of a Roman villa. In the early seventeenth century James I replaced the fence with a brick wall, which cost £2,000 for its two-mile length. Later in the same century Andre Le Notre (1613-1700), Louis XIV's gardener, laid out the park with avenues of trees. Separating the park from the former gardens of the Queen's House are sunken flowerbeds, which were originally part of the haha (a ditch used as a boundary to avoid the use of walls, fences, or hedgerows). Another relic of Tudor days is Queen Elizabeth's oak, round which Elizabeth I's parents, Henry VIII and Anne Boleyn, are said to have danced. Later, according to legend, the tree's hollow stump was used as a lockup for persons who broke the regulations of the park. Many other trees in the grounds are centuries old and are the delight of arboriculturists. The park was first open to the public in the eighteenth century.

On the top of the hill in the park stands the **statue of General Wolfe** (9), by Tait MacKenzie. Wolfe (1727-59) was the conqueror of the Heights of Abraham at Quebec in Canada and lies buried in the parish church of Greenwich.

**Flamstead House** (10), named after the first Astronomer Royal, the Rev. John Flamsteed, housed the **Royal Observatory** from 1675 until 1948, when it was moved to Herstmonceux Castle in East Sussex. It was built on the foundations of the watch-tower of Humphrey, Duke of Gloucester, its cost being defrayed with money obtained from the sale of some old decayed gunpowder. It still stands sentinel over Greenwich from the highest point of the park. It was on this spot that the Duke erected a castle in 1428 and which was in use until the building of the observatory. Today the house is an extension of the National Maritime Museum and is devoted to astronomy and navigation. In the Octagon Room are several clocks by Thomas Tompion (1639-1713), the father of English clockmaking. In 1965 His Royal Highness Prince Philip, Duke of Edinburgh, inaugurated the Caird Planetarium nearby.

By an international agreement of 1884 in Washington, USA, the **meridian of zero longitude** runs through Greenwich and is marked by a brass strip on the ground. Like latitude, whose zero line is the Equator, longitude measurements are the means of location from the base line.

Sir John Vanbrugh (1664-1726), soldier, architect and playwright, designed for himself a house on Maze Hill (11). Known today as **Vanbrugh's Castle,** it is modelled on the former Parisian prison, the Bastille, where Sir John was imprisoned between 1690 and 1692 on the charge of spying for the British Government. There is a blue plaque on the outside wall of the grounds of the house.

In the past hundred years or so the **Trafalgar Tavern** (12), in Park Road, has served as a place of refreshment, a home for aged seamen, living quarters for members of the Royal Navy, and a men's club. The site was previously occupied by the George Tavern and there is mention of this building in the eleventh century. Charles Dickens (1812-70) mentioned the tavern in *Our mutual friend* and here he met for the last time the author Douglas Jerrold (1803-57), whose successful plays included *Black-ey'd Susan* from the ballad by John Gay. The present building was built in 1837 to the designs of Joseph Kay (1775-1847), who was Surveyor to Greenwich Hospital at the time. A pupil of Samuël Pepys Cockerell, Kay became the secretary of the Architects Club and a founder member of the Institute of British Architects. He was also responsible for the layout of Nelson Street in Greenwich in 1829. Whitebait, once caught in the river nearby, is a speciality of the house and may well have been on the menu at the last Liberal Dinner here to be presided over by William Gladstone in 1883.

In Crane Street by the river you will find the **Yacht public house** (13), which has stood here for over three hundred years. Stones engraved with seventeenth-century masons' marks have been found near here, where one can watch the river and its history flow by. The Greenwich meridian line runs through the building, adding another unusual touch to the place.

Near the Yacht is the **Trinity Hospital** (14), almshouses founded in 1613 by Henry Howard, first Earl of Northampton, for twelve men of Greenwich and eight from Shottisham in Suffolk, the Earl's birthplace. His father Henry Howard, Earl of Surrey

(1517-47), had been executed on a charge of treason, and the son found no favour in the court of Elizabeth I;he was arrested in 1571 on the charge of aspiring to marry Mary Stuart. The title lapsed on his death in 1614 and he was buried in the tiny chapel, where his kneeling figure, clad in armour, can still be seen.

---

# 7. Hammersmith

Originally built in 1864 slightly to the north of its present position, the Metropolitan Line **underground station** (1) was rebuilt four years later on the present site. From the corner of the road here it is possible to see the District and Piccadilly Lines station; it was first constructed in 1874 but had to be rebuilt after a fire in 1882. Note the titles of the railway companies which formerly operated their services here.

Hammersmith is first mentioned in the thirteenth century and the name is said to derive from either a 'home', or town, with a hithe — a small dock built into the bank of the river — or from a smithy, with the 'hammer' and 'smythe' joining to become the town's own name. In its present spelling the name is recorded in a document of 1675.

Using the subway, cross to the opposite side of the road. On the corner of Hammersmith Broadway and Hammersmith Road stands the **Convent of the Sacred Heart** (2), designed by John Bentley, the architect of Westminster Cathedral. It dates from 1876 and, as well as the nuns, houses two schools for Roman Catholic children. It is not open to the public but it does show Bentley's work at its best.

Turn away from the convent to the Butterwick, now the local bus station; its name comes from the manor house which still stands round the corner opposite the church. Continuing through the bus station, the road leads towards the Hammersmith Flyover and round two corners to the entrance to the Hammersmith bus depot; standing between the entrance doorways is the former manor house of the **Butterwick** (3), built in the seventeenth century.

To cross the road safely find the subway, by the nearby underground station, and take the left-hand exit up to the **church of St Paul** (4). The present building was erected in 1882 to the designs of Roumieu, Gough and Seddon but it contains several items from previous centuries. The font dates from the seventeenth century, as do the chairs in the chancel, while the pulpit, designed by Sir Christopher Wren, came from the church of All Hallows, Thames Street, in the City of London. Monuments worth noting include one to Sir Nicholas Crisp, a Royalist at the time of the Civil War. He helped Charles I raise an army and had inscribed on his monument, erected during his lifetime, the words 'that glorious martyr King Charles the First of blessed memory'. There is also a monument to Sir Samuel Morland, the inventor of a water pump for use in Windsor Castle.

Leave the churchyard by the south-east corner and the flyover is immediately overhead. Pass underneath and the car park of the National Car Parks Company (5) is on the right. By crossing over the park Hammersmith Bridge Road is reached.

Opposite is a public house, the **Oxford and Cambridge** (6), appropriately situated by the road that leads to the river and one of the best vantage points for watching the Boat Race — Hammersmith Bridge.

To the side of the roadway are the **Digby Mansions** (7); on the side of the approach wall to the bridge an old public drinking fountain can be seen, though no longer in working order.

It is not far from the fountain to the riverbank, from where we can take a look at **Hammersmith Bridge** (8). Designed by Sir Joseph Bazalgette, who also engineered the Thames embankments, it was built in 1884-7 and replaces the earlier bridge, built in 1827 by Tierney Clark, which was the first suspension bridge over the Thames. The later bridge uses the piers of its predecessor to support its towers. On the wooden handrail on the upstream side of the bridge is a small metal plaque recording the gallant deed of Charles Wood, an officer in the Royal Air Force who saved a drowning woman by diving from the bridge. The coats of arms on the bridge are the arms of Guildford, Kent, Middlesex and the former Metropolitan Board of Works.

The riverside walk here is called the **Lower Mall** (9) and leads from the bridge past Hammersmith Pier to the Dove public house. Almost immediately you will come to a short row of eighteenth-century houses: No. 6 is the headquarters of the Amateur Rowing Association and No. 10 is a fine example of the style of Robert Adam, though not actually designed by him. Note the very fine doorway and the wrought iron railings and gate. Among the riverside taverns here are the Blue Anchor and the Rutland, which displays that family's coat of arms.

The **Furnivall Gardens** (10), whose name commemorates one of the borough's great benefactors, occupy the site that until 1936 was Hammersmith Creek. A few yards from the river stands **Westcott Lodge** (11); now owned by the local authority and used as a community centre, it was once the vicarage. The old-fashioned lamp holder on the side of the house once lit a street in West Berlin; it was presented to the borough by Willy Brandt as a symbol of the friendship between the two places.

**Hammersmith Pier** (12), also dating from the filling in of the old creek, is widely used during the summer by the boats that take visitors on trips up and down the Thames. Across the gardens can

# HAMMERSMITH

1 Underground station
2 Convent of the Sacred Heart
3 Butterwick manor house
4 St Paul's church
5 Car park
6 The Oxford and Cambridge
7 Digby Mansions
8 Hammersmith Bridge
9 Lower Mall
10 Furnivall Gardens
11 Westcott Lodge
12 Hammersmith Pier
13 Doves Bindery

14 The Dove
15 Kelmscott House
16 Rivercourt Road
17 Linden House
18 Oil Mill Lane
19 Hammersmith Pumping Station
20 The Black Lion
21 Hammersmith Terrace
22 St Peter's church
23 St Peter's Square
24 Ravenscourt Park
25 St John's church

be seen Hammersmith Town Hall; its rebuilding started in the late 1930s but the modern extensions, on the King Street side, were opened in 1970. On the other side of the river can be seen the new St Paul's School. The school was founded in the sixteenth century by Dean Colet for 153 poor boys. At first it was housed in the churchyard of St Paul's Cathedral but it occupied a site in Hammersmith Road from 1885 until it moved to its present site.

It is a short walk to the other half of Hammersmith's Mall, the Upper Mall, and to step back into the atmosphere of the seventeenth and eighteenth centuries. No.15 has two inscriptions on it recording that the **Doves Bindery** (13) and private printing press were here and that Thomas Sanderson lived here.

The **Dove public house** (14), dating from the seventeenth century, has much to offer the passer-by both in history and in refreshment. The pub is mentioned in a number of literary works.

Next along the Mall is **Kelmscott House** (15), dating from the 1780s. William Morris lived here from 1878 to 1896, using the stables for holding meetings. He set up a tapestry loom in one of

31

the bedrooms, and the Kelmscott Press, a famous private press of the period, was set up in the cottage of No. 14. Some of the rooms in the house are still decorated with wallpaper designed by Morris.

**Rivercourt Road** (16), leading down to the river, is a reminder of the court that ruled over the river in days long ago.

Continuing along the Upper Mall past the eighteenth-century house used by Latymer School, we come to **Linden House** (17), a Queen Anne style house and the home of the London Corinthian Sailing Club. Just beyond the house is a short arcade under the modern houses built slightly nearer the river than the other buildings we have already seen.

Turn away from the river to the side of Linden House and the path takes the explorer to the busy Great West Road, passing a collection of houses of the nineteenth and twentieth centuries in **Oil Mill Lane** (18).

At the junction of this quiet backwater and the busy dual carriageway turn left and shortly the waterworks appears. Belonging to the Thames Water Authority, the **Hammersmith Pumping Station** (19) delivers 45 million gallons (200 million litres) of water each day to the West End and west London. The building dates from 1811 and was designed by W. Tierney Clark, architect of the previous Hammersmith Bridge. The building incorporates a seventeenth-century structure which may have been a riverside gatehouse for one of the great houses that stood here then. It is just possible that the gate was the one that led to the house of Charles II's widow, Catharine of Braganza, whose gardens were mentioned by John Evelyn in his diary.

Passing the waterworks on the left, continue to walk along the pavement of the Great West Road until a signpost directs towards Terrace Villas, Western Terrace, Montrose Villas and Mulberry Place, pointing along South Black Lion Lane. At the end of the lane is the **Black Lion** public house (20), a pleasant nineteenth-century house, with a friendly welcome inside.

Looking through the open space on the left we can see the modern riverside houses mentioned when considering Linden House. But at this junction can be found **Hammersmith Terrace** (21), a set of sixteen identical houses whose front doors open straight on to the pavement, while their backs look directly on to the river. The noted Royal Academician Philip de Loutherbourg lived in Nos. 7 and 8 in the late eighteenth century; while here he was 'taken to prophecy and healing', an activity which greatly amused Walpole, who made him a subject of a number of his letters. A later resident of No. 7 was Sir Emery Walker, the typographer and friend of William Morris. He and Morris founded the Kelmscott Press. His house is now marked with a blue plaque.

Shortly after Sir Emery's house the Hammersmith Upper Mall

joins with the Chiswick Mall and we must leave the riverside walk and, turning right, follow the course of the road, Eyot Gardens, back to the Great West Road. Here turn right, back towards the centre of Hammersmith, passing Verbena Gardens, and walking to the subway under the Great West Road. Use the subway to reach **St Peter's church** (22). The church was built between 1827 and 1829 and is the oldest church in Hammersmith. Its architect, Edward Lapidge, was an assistant to the famous landscape designer Lancelot 'Capability' Brown and later became the County Surveyor for Surrey. It is built of yellow bricks and its chief glory is the Ionic porch at the west end. Many of the fittings are original and have been well preserved from modern innovations.

**St Peter's Square** (23) was described by one architectural historian as being like a suburban Belgravia. Built between 1825 and 1830, it does give an impression of that fashionable district, though on a smaller scale.

Leave the square by way of St Peter's Villas, which road joins Black Lion Lane. By turning left into the lane King Street is reached. This is the busy high street of Hammersmith and there is much to see, but we shall make a pleasant diversion into **Ravenscourt Park** (24). The manor of Pallenswick was granted to Alice Perrers, the mistress of Edward III, in 1373, but after her banishment five years later the property was seized by the crown. In 1813 a document refers to the ownership of the house by George Scott and describes it as being the 'manor house lately called Ravenscourt'. The public park was opened in 1888, covering 34 acres (14 hectares), with pleasant paths, lawns and an old English garden.

Return to King Street and walk along to Studland Road. Turn left and soon, after passing under the District and Piccadilly Lines railway bridge, turn right into Glenthorne Road. The continual growth of population in the nineteenth century made it necessary to build many new churches to accommodate all the people. One of the newer churches of Hammersmith is **St John's church** (25), which was built in 1859 to the designs of William Butterfield.

It is a short walk from here to Beadon Road, which leads to Hammersmith Broadway and the Metropolitan Line station.

---

# 8. Hampstead

**Hampstead Underground station** (1) is the deepest in London's system, being 192 feet below the surface. Using the Northern Line of the Underground railway it is possible today to leave the City of London and in half an hour arrive at Hampstead, but less than a century ago this would not have been possible.

First mentioned in a charter of King Edgar in 957, the manor of Hampstead is recorded in 986 as having been given by Ethelred to Westminster Abbey, who owned it until 1550 and the Dissolution of the abbey. By the seventeenth century there were a few houses, and merchants from the City moved their families here to flee from plague-ridden London, commuting each day by horse or coach. In a gazetteer published in 1880 Hampstead is given as being four miles from London.

The name Hampstead means 'a homestead' or 'farm' but it is not known when the 'p' crept in.

**Church Row** (2) has been described by many authorities as the best street in Hampstead. A variety of houses of the eighteenth century are to be seen here, and on one of them is a plaque commemorating John James Park (1795-1833), the author of a history of Hampstead.

In the churchyard of the parish church, **Saint John's** (3), can be found many famous names engraved on the tombstones. Explorers who know that the main entrance to a church is the west door and that the altars, or holy tables, are always at the east, should be warned that this church is not correctly orientated - look up at the weathervane and you will see. Tucked away in the south-east corner of the churchyard lie John Constable (1776-1837), the artist, his wife and some of their children. A few yards south of the church wall can be seen the grave of John Harrison (1693-1776), the inventor of the chronometer. Across the road - Church Row - is the extension to the churchyard. Here, near to the railings, can be seen the graves of Hugh Gaitskell (1903-63), Leader of the Labour Party from 1955; Kay Kendall (Harrison), actress; Anton Walbrook, actor; and George Du Maurier, illustrator.

In 1816 the Abbé Morel, with a group of French refugees, settled in Hampstead and built a church, which they dedicated to Saint Mary. Today the interior of **Saint Mary's** (4) comes as a pleasant surprise to the explorer of Hampstead. The statue of the Blessed Virgin Mary is a model of the statue that overlooks Buenos Aires, the capital of Argentina. The founder's tomb is just inside the door, a mark in the linoleum showing the spot.

Halfway up a flight of steps which lead from Heath Street to Holly Mount is **Golden Yard** (5). Dating from the seventeenth century, the delightful houses in this little courtyard make the diversion from the main road well worthwhile.

A charming little cul-de-sac, **Holly Mount** (6), once possessed a chapel, now No. 17, in which John Wesley is believed to have preached.

Turn right at the top of Holly Bush Hill and you will find the **Holly Bush public house** (7). Built in 1643, its sign reminds one of the custom of hanging a green branch or bush, by way of advertisement, outside a house licensed to sell ale. Once connected

# HAMPSTEAD

1 Hampstead Underground station
2 Church Row
3 Saint John's Church and churchyard
4 Saint Mary's Catholic church
5 Golden Yard
6 Holly Mount (former chapel)
7 Holly Bush public house
8 Romney's House
9 Bolton House
10 Fenton House
11 Old and New Grove Houses
12 Admiral's House
13 Whitestone Pond
14 Vale of Health
15 Jack Straw's Castle
16 Hampstead Heath
17 Leg of Mutton Pond
18 Spaniards Inn

with the house next door, Romney's House, when it was used as the Constitutional Club, today it provides a quiet haven away from the hustle and bustle of modern life. Visitors to the tavern have included Marie Lloyd, 'Two-ton' Tessie O'Shea, Dr Samuel Johnson and James Boswell, Oliver Goldsmith, Leigh Hunt and Charles Lamb.

**Romney's House** (8) was bought by George Romney, the famous portrait artist, in 1796 for £700, with rates of £50 per year. The house had been built originally at the turn of the eighteenth century and was complete with stables when Romney moved in. His first task was to have the stables removed, for although he was fond of horse-riding he did not like riding in public, and he had an indoor studio built instead, with a gallery and living room attached. A side entrance led to the gallery, where he entertained his mistresses. After Romney left the house and resold it, the brewer at the Holly Bush bought it and turned the house into the Hampstead Constitutional Club, linking it, by a specially made door, to the tavern round the corner. Later the house was divided into two as a private house - and so it remains. There are no paintings by Romney in the house today.

Across the green formed by the junction of Holly Bush Hill, Frognal Rise and Hampstead Grove stands **Bolton House** (9), with its commemorative plaque announcing that Joanna Brillie (1762-1851), the Scottish poetess and dramatist, lived in the house. Walter Scott was a frequent visitor to the house and once wrote to the effect that he looked forward to visiting it. Joanna's tragedies are described as the best written by any woman of the period. John Kemble, the actor-manager, and his sister Sarah Siddons acted in some of her plays.

**Fenton House** (10) is an excellent example of a late seventeenth-century Hampstead house, the date 1693 being painted on a plaque over the entrance. The identity of the architect is unknown, but Sir Christopher Wren has been suggested; neither is it known who the original owner was. In the early eighteenth century it is listed as Ostend House but by 1786 had become known as Clock House - whether there was a clock on the outside wall nobody seems to be sure. A certain P. I. Fenton bought the house in 1793 and as Fenton House it has been known ever since. The National Trust now owns the house, which houses the Benton Fletcher Collection of keyboard instruments and the Benning Collection of porcelain and furniture. The latter collection was part of the estate, given to the Trust with the house in 1936 by the late Lady Benning, the owner. A painting in the Morning Room, by John Constable, shows Hampstead Heath in the eighteenth century.

Belonging to the eighteenth century are **Old and New Grove Houses** (11). In the latter lived the architect Henry Flitcroft (1679-1769), while in the former, as a brown plaque on the wall records, lived the Du Maurier family.

George IV had an admiral by the name of Barton, who when he retired from the sea, came to live in Hampstead, in what is **Admiral's House** (12) today. He converted the roof into a quarterdeck of a ship and, on 'high feasts and holydays' raised the White Ensign and fired his cannon in celebration. Constable painted the house in his picture *The romantic house of Hampstead,* which is in the Tate Gallery in London. A plaque on the wall tells of George Gilbert Scott, architect (1811-78), and his family living here in the nineteenth century, but they found it too cold in the winter and moved back into London. In the cottage to the side of the house lived John Galsworthy (1867-1933), the author of *The Forsyte saga.*

Mr Pickwick delivered a lecture to the members of the Pickwick Club on the subject of the source of the Hampstead Ponds. The flagpole at **Whitestone Pond** (13) marks the highest spot in the London area - 440 feet above sea-level. Opposite the pond is the village pound, where stray animals were kept until redeemed by their owners. There is an inscription on a stone which reads *'Anno 1787'.*

The **Vale of Health** (14) is one of a number of small hamlets round about Hampstead Heath. Leigh Hunt (1784-1859) came in 1816 to live here and extols its beauty in his poems. He lived in one of the earliest cottages in the Vale which, alas, has long since been pulled down to make way for less suitable buildings. It was after having stayed with Hunt that Keats, too, took a great liking to Hampstead and became a resident in Wentworth Place from 1817 to 1820.

A favourite walk of Charles Dickens, we are told, was across Hampstead Heath to a meal at **Jack Straw's Castle** (15) - not that he saw the present building, as it was rebuilt after the Second World War. Whether the name comes from a certain Jack Straw, a ringleader in the Peasants' Revolt of 1381, or from a Jane Straw who once lived here, is still being debated in all its bars. Other recorded visitors include Thackeray, Robert Louis Stevenson, Wilkie Collins and John Forster, biographer of Dickens. In the eighteenth century horse-races took place behind the inn but attracted undesirable elements and were closed down in the same century. It was also the meeting place of the Court Leet of the manor of Hampstead.

**Hampstead Heath** (16) is one of the few remaining wild pieces of open space in the London area - others include Wimbledon Common and Epping Forest. Comprising over eight hundred acres today, the original public purchase was East, West and Sandy Heaths in 1871. Gradually over the next hundred years other land was acquired. Except at bank holiday fair time the heath offers peace and quiet with miles of paths for pleasant walks. Like other open spaces the Heath has memories of highwaymen. Tales are told of Dick Turpin and his famous ride to York and of Jackson who in 1673 was hanged for highway murder behind Jack Straw's Castle.

**Leg of Mutton Pond** (17) was dug before 1825 by unemployed poor of the parish.

Originally built in the seventeenth century, the **Spaniards Inn** (18) was at the entrance to the Bishop of London's park. The tollhouse opposite is now scheduled as an ancient monument. The inn has strong literary and historical connections. Dick Turpin's fictional ride from York mentions the Spaniards, and there is a display of keys and pistols said to have belonged to the highwayman, together with leg-irons used to secure him in Newgate. Dickens uses the place as the scene of a tea-party for Mrs Bardell in *Pickwick papers* and of her arrest in her breach of promise case against Pickwick. At the time of the Gordon Riots (1780-1), the inn's landlord, Giles Thomas, detained the rioters who were on their way to wreck the home of Lord Mansfield, Kenwood. He succeeded in diverting their attention long enough to allow an ostler to rouse a party of the Horse Guards who suitably detained them.

How the tavern acquired its name is open to conjecture, but there are two possible suggestions: that the house was once occupied by members of the Spanish embassy staff and so become known as the Spaniards' House; alternatively that the tavern was owned by two Spanish brothers in the eighteenth century, but they both fell in love with the same woman and fought a duel in the yard of the inn. When the winner returned to the house the woman had disappeared. He then returned to the yard and buried his brother there.

---

# 9. Highgate

With its spire pointing towards the sky, Saint Michael's Church, Highgate, stands on London's Northern Heights. Seen from a distance it reminds one of the existence of a tiny village now completely absorbed by the metropolis.

Riding along on the crest of the hill, Highgate is 424 feet above the river Thames, and, looking out over towards the City of London, one is standing above the level of the cross on the top of Saint Paul's Cathedral. Although Hampstead Heath is some twenty feet higher than the village, it does not appear so when wandering on it. Perhaps it is the steepness of the descents on three sides, the north face being the only one which remains fairly level for some distance, that gives the impression of a greater height here at Highgate.

## HIGHGATE

1 Coleridge's house
2 Reservoir
3 Gatehouse Tavern
4 Highgate School
5 Pond Square
6 The Flask tavern
7 Saint Michael's Church
8 Highgate Cemetery

9 Waterlow Park
10 Statue of Sir Sydney Waterlow
11 Lauderdale House
12 Site of Andrew Marvell's house
13 Cromwell House
14 Saint Joseph's Catholic church
15 Archway
16 Whittington's Stone

Opposite the church, at **No. 3 The Grove** (1), lived Samuel Taylor Coleridge (1772-1834), the poet and literary critic, born in the vicarage of Ottery St Mary, Devon. He was educated at Christ's Hospital, London (a plaque in Newgate Street in the City marks the spot where the school was founded) and later studied at Jesus College, Cambridge. He spent the last eighteen years of his life living with James Gillman in Highgate and on his death in July 1834 was buried in the burial ground of the old school chapel. The Gillmans erected a memorial to him in the church, the first to be placed in the new building, and in 1961 his body, together with those of his daughter, Sara, and her husband, were reinterred in the church. The first six houses of The Grove were erected between 1682 and 1685 but the Gillmans' house is the least altered of the set of semi-detached houses, which appear to have been built to a single specification.

At the end of the sixteenth century, John Norden in his *Speculum Britanniae* wrote: 'upon this hill is a most pleasant dwelling'. He was referring to Dorchester House, in the garden of which now stand the houses of The Grove. The home of Henry, Lord Marquess of Dorchester, the house was to have been a charity school for girls under a plan set up by the son of a local resident, William Blake, who was described by Lysons in his *Environs of London*, published in 1791, as being 'a crazy philanthropist, a woolen draper at the sign of the Golden Boy in Maiden Lane, Covent Garden'. The children were to be 'decently cloathed in blew, lined with yellow; constanly fed all alike with good wholsom diet, taught to read, write, and cast accompts (accounts), and so put out to trades, in order to live another day'. Unfortunately Blake did not receive the financial support that he had hoped for, and the school came to an abrupt end in 1685, by which time the houses of The Grove had been built.

It seems that Highgate Grove or Green was the recognised place for all the local revelries and fairs to take place up to the eighteenth century. Here, in July 1744, at the time of the Highgate Fair, a sack race was organised when the landlord gave a pair of gloves as a prize. A pig was to be turned loose on the Wednesday of the fair and 'who ever catches it by the tail, throws it over his head, shall have it'. Surrounded by elms of great beauty and age, the green must have presented an attractive sight in days gone by. Before leaving The Grove look back and admire **Widanhurst,** built in the style of William and Mary, with a west wing dating from the early eighteenth century.

The provision of drinking water has always been a problem of supply and demand and the presence of an **underground reservoir** here (2) reminds one of the need today. This portion of South Grove contains a number of houses of the eighteenth and nineteenth centuries which are worth noting.

Lysons quotes the fact that the setting up of a 'gate upon the hill' gives the village its name. Today the **Gatehouse Tavern** (3), standing on the borders of the former parishes of Hornsey and St Pancras, has little to commend it architecturally, but its name refers to the fact that here, in the Middle Ages, stood one of the three gatehouse entrances to the 'Greate Park of Haringhey, alias Hornsey', belonging to the Bishops of London. The other two entrances were at the Spaniards, Hampstead, and at Newgate, near East Finchley railway station; nothing remains today of either.

Nearby, too, was the 'high-gate', the first tollgate to be erected in England, and which was guarded by the hermit of Highgate. This same man constructed the pond and, when his own private resources ceased, was ordered by the king, Edward III (1312-77), to set up the bar across the road here; the tolls from this helped to pay for the building of the road of the 'Hollow-way'.

There are a number of inns in the area, including the Gatehouse, which are connected with the old custom of 'swearing on the horns'. This ancient practice takes place twice a year when, for a small fee that is donated to a local charity, anyone interested can become a 'Freeman' of Highgate.

Before the London Government Act of 1963 the Gatehouse inn lay half in Hornsey, then in the former county of Middlesex, and half in the borough of St Pancras. In previous times the Middlesex Sessions were held in an old courtroom on the second floor, and the London side of the room was roped off to make sure that the prisoners did not escape to another authority's area.

In 1565 Sir Roger Cholmeley founded the 'Free Grammar School of Sir Roger Cholmeley', the chapel of which stood on the site of the former hermitage of Saint Michael. Old Highgate was never a parish in its own right but the chapel developed into being virtually a chapel of ease, that is a place for public worship for the use of parishioners living a distance from the parish church, for the parishes of both Hornsey and St Pancras, as well as being the school chapel. However, a judgement in 1826 in the Court of Chancery, one of the three divisions of the High Court of Justice, ruled that the public had no right to be there, and with the re-endowment of the school its chapel reverted to private use. The school buildings were rebuilt in 1819 and the statutes remodelled in 1824. Today **Highgate School** (4) is a flourishing one of public-school standards and has several hundred boys on its roll. A number of old monuments from the school chapel have been re-erected in Saint Michael's Parish Church. The old chapel of the school was demolished in 1833, when the present one in the early French Gothic style took its place, while in the 1860s further rebuilding of the school premises replaced older structures, but the old burial ground on the corner of Southwood Lane remains as a reminder of its past association with the parish.

**Southwood Lane,** picturesque and winding, contains Southwood House, dating from 1746 with a porch added later in the same century. Also in the lane are the Woolaston-Paunceforth Almshouses, rebuilt in the third decade of the eighteenth century.

A short walk down the High Street, with its many interesting shops and houses, is **South Grove** in which there are several buildings worth the attention of the architectural student. It was while staying at Arundel House, whose site is now occupied by Old Hall, that Francis Bacon (1561-1626), philosopher, writer, and a contender for the privilege of having written Shakespeare's plays, died. His death was caused, according to tradition, through a chill he had caught while experimenting with a primitive form of refrigeration by stuffing a fowl with snow.

Forming part of the original, much larger village green is **Pond Square** (5); its Georgian cottages were an early encroachment on an area dedicated to entertainment in medieval days. The pond itself has long since disappeared and asphalt has taken the place of water. In his book *Worthies of England* Dr Thomas Fuller (1608-61) compliments the hermit of Highgate for excavating

41

Highgate Pond, so providing a hollow at the top of the hill to catch water in, and for using the gravel out of the pit to construct a causeway in the Hollow-way (Holloway Road) to take travellers safely on their way to the City of London. It is said that the square is haunted by the chicken which was stuffed with snow by Francis Bacon.

No village scene is complete without its pub and Highgate's is called **The Flask** (6). Although opinions vary as to the exact date of the first tavern on this site, all agree that the present building is late seventeenth-century. The inn was the meeting place in the eighteenth century of a number of distinguished artists, amongst whom was William Hogarth (1697-1764), who witnessed the quarrel between two drinkers that resulted in one felling the other by striking him with a pint pot. The look on the stricken man's face turned from anguish to a hideous grin, and Hogarth quickly sketched the scene to the amusement of both men. There are also a number of stories told that link Dick Turpin with the Flask and tell how, on one occasion, he jumped the nearby high-gate with Black Bess when being pursued - or did he merely hide in the cellars? The Flask is also linked with the custom of swearing on the horns, and some authorities claim that the practice originated here with graziers bringing their cattle from the Midlands to Smithfield. They formed themselves into a fraternity, entry to which required the applicant to take an oath and kiss the horns - perhaps originally on the ox itself. Strange as it may seem, the name of the inn comes from the fact that water from the nearby Hampstead Wells was sold here in the eighteenth century, in flasks. Another visitor in the eighteenth century was Major Robert Rogers, who discovered the land route to the North-west Passage of North America. Rogers's Rangers have a place in the history of America as a band of frontiersmen who fought with British troops during the French-Indian war between 1756 and 1763. In the American War of Independence (1775-6) there was a justifiable doubt as to where Rogers's loyalties lay and both sides rejected his services. On his return to Britain he settled in London, where he died in 1795.

Standing on one of the highest points of the northern heights is the parish church of Highgate, **Saint Michael's** (7), which was designed by Lewis Vulliamy (1791-1871) in 1830, with a chancel added by George Edmund Street (1824-81) in the year of his death. Vulliamy, the son of Benjamin Vulliamy the clockmaker, designed several London churches, including the now demolished Christ Church, Woburn Square, but is perhaps best known for Dorchester House in Park Lane, which was demolished in 1929 to make way for the Dorchester Hotel. The cost of the church was borne equally by the Church Commissioners and the parishioners and amounted to £10,000. On the site once stood Ashurst House, shown on early maps as the Mansion House and built for Sir William Ashurst, Lord Mayor of London in 1694. The house was demolished in 1830 to make way for the church.

On the southern slopes of the hill, to the east of Saint Michael's Church, lies **Highgate Cemetery** (8), laid out in 1838 by David Ramsay, who was the London Cemetery Company's landscape gardener. Incorporated by an Act of Parliament, the company's task was to establish private cemeteries in the northern, eastern and southern suburbs of London. The entrance to the older portion of the cemetery, in Swain Lane, was the work of Stephen Geary (c 1797-1854), who is chiefly known for his work of laying out cemeteries in the nineteenth century, 'an architect whose taste and ability have been long and justly appreciated'. Directly below Saint Michael's Church are the catacombs, with their Egyptian-style portal and vaults dug into the side of the hill; through the open doors of some may be seen the coffins resting on their shelves. This portion of the cemetery is dominated by the mausoleum of Julius Beer, with a stepped pyramid as its top, in the form of the mausoleum of Halicarnassus, designed by John Oldrid Scott (1841-1913), the second son of Sir George Gilbert Scott, with interior sculpture by Henry Armstead. The cemetery today, with its extension of 1855, contains the graves of some 45,000 people. Amongst them is Karl Marx (1818-83), whose book *Das Kapital,* the first volume of which was published in 1867, was used by Lenin as a basis for the teaching and development of communism, and which led to the formation of the Union of Soviet Socialist Republics in 1917. Here too are the parents of Charles Dickens; George Eliot (1819-80), whose real name was Mary Ann Evans and who was the author of such novels as *Adam Bede, The mill on the Floss* and *Felix Holt;* Sir Rowland Hill (1795-1879), who in 1840 introduced the Penny Post; Tom Sayers (1825-65), a famous boxer; Michael Faraday (1791-1867), the British chemist and physicist whose work in the field of electricity brought into use the magneto and dynamo machines; John Frederick Denison Maurice (1805-72), founder of the Working Man's College at Camden Town and a great leader in the field of socialism in the nineteenth century. A memorial inscription reads: 'William Friese-Greene, inventor of kinematography. His genius bestowed upon humanity the boon of commercial kinematography, of which he was the first inventor and patentee.' Friese-Green (1855-1921) first showed moving pictures in public in 1890, at No. 20 Brooke Street, Holborn.

Sir Sydney Waterlow gave twenty-six acres of land to Londoners in 1889, and two years later **Waterlow Park** (9) was open to the public. The park has many attractions, including two ponds with a wide variety of waterfowl, an aviary, quiet gardens and, during the summer months, a grass theatre where drama, opera and ballet are performed.

The **statue of Sir Sydney Waterlow** (10), Lord Mayor of London 1872-3, was erected in his memory with money collected, mainly from the poor of the district, in 1900. Collecting boxes in the park realised as much as £18 in one day, and all in coins of less than one shilling. In Sir Sydney's right hand are an umbrella and trilby hat made of stone, and this is the only statue in London to depict these items in this way.

Standing within the grounds of Waterlow Park is **Lauderdale House** (11), dating from the sixteenth century, with additions in the seventeenth and eighteenth centuries. It belonged to the second Earl (later Duke) of Lauderdale (1616-82). While the Earl was in Scotland, Charles II installed Nell Gwynne in the house, and it is said that on one occasion when the king was passing by Nell held a child out of an upstairs window by a leg and called to Charles: 'Name this child'. To this the king replied: 'God save the Earl of Burford'. It should be added that this story is repeated elsewhere in the kingdom but the earldom changes with the place! Samuel Pepys (1633-1703), the diarist, records a visit to the house in July 1666, when he listened to one of the servants playing a violin and to Lord Lauderdale reflecting on his hatred of music, particularly the lute and bagpipe.

By leaving Lauderdale House by its front gates, turning left and walking a short way up Highgate High Street there can be found a **plaque** (12) marking the site of the cottage in which lived Andrew Marvell (1621-78), the poet and assistant to John Milton in the Latin secretaryship to the Council, and later member of Parliament for Hull.

On the opposite side of the roadway to the Marvell plaque is the misnamed **Cromwell House** (13); although the house is contemporary with the Lord Protector, having been built in 1630, there is no direct evidence that he ever lived in it at any time of his life. Perhaps it was the carved newel posts of the staircase that gave rise to the suggestion that General Ireton, son-in-law to Oliver Cromwell, lived in the house. However, according to the London Survey Committee researching the house and its history, both these suggestions are baseless. John Ireton, the general's brother, obtained possession of Lauderdale House in 1651 and lived there until the Restoration of the monarchy in 1660 when the Earl of Lauderdale's property was restored to him.

In reply to the Anglican domination of the skyline with Saint Michael's Church, the Roman Catholic church of **Saint Joseph's** (14) matches well from the other side of Waterlow Park and can be seen from a comparable distance. The church was built in 1875-6 in the Italianate style by Tasker.

Highgate Hill has always proved a formidable proposition for heavy traffic, in spite of the fact that the road was on gravel and would therefore stay firm even in the wettest of conditions. However, early in the nineteenth century plans were made for an alternative road to be constructed with a lesser incline. After an abortive attempt to build a tunnel through the hill, a deep cutting was made, on the recommendation of Sir John Rennie (1794-1874), the second son of John Rennie, the bridge-builder and civil engineer. This new road cut off two portions of Hornsey Lane, and John Nash (1752-1835) designed the first **Archway** (15) over the new road. Its steel successor, designed by Sir Alexander Binnie, Chief Engineer of the London County Council, in 1897 affords an excellent view from these Northern Heights across the sprawling metropolis and towards the City of London.

Returning from Archway to Saint Joseph's Church, the walker will find himself at the top of Highgate Hill. With the view of London before him, he can well imagine the bells of the City pealing out their messages of welcome over the past hundreds of years. Standing on the roadside on Highgate Hill is the stone known as **Whittington's Stone** (16). It is said to have been here when young Richard Whittington (c 1358-1423), later four times Lord Mayor of London, feeling despondent, left London to return to Gloucester. (Quite how he planned to do this is a puzzle to many people for, Gloucester being in the West, one would have thought that this place was on the wrong road. However, the story-books and the pantomimes tell us that he rested here, where he heard the bells of Saint Mary-le-Bow, in Cheapside, ring out a 'message' for him: 'Turn again Whittington, thrice Lord Mayor of London'. He did return to the City and, later became Lord Mayor. The present stone dates from 1821 and replaces the original one, which is believed to have been the base of a wayside cross, that had been removed in the eighteenth century and placed at the end of Queen's Head Lane.

In the reign of Edward IV, William Poole fell ill with leprosy and founded a hospital, a lazar-house, near where the Whittington stone is today on Highgate Hill. The wayside cross referred to above was outside the hospital. In his will Richard Cloudesley left 6s 8d 'to the poor lazars of Hyegate', to pray for him by name in their bede-roll.

# 10. Islington

Before the coming of the Romans this area was covered by the great Forest of Middlesex but later developed as 'the hill or down of Gisla', as shown in the Anglo-Saxon Chronicle, into a village around the Upper and Lower Roads. Today these streets, the latter renamed Essex Road, meet at Islington Green.

Starting at Angel underground station (Northern Line) it is a short walk to the **Angel** (1), once a famous coaching inn and later an equally famous Lyons Corner House teashop. Here we turn right into the High Street that leads us towards the Upper and Lower Streets. Weekday walkers will find much to distract them from their purpose of exploring the former village, for there are shops and an open air market, as well as the Camden Passage Antiques just beyond the Green.

One of the most impressive buildings by the Green is the former **Royal Agricultural Hall** (2), built in 1862 by the Smithfield Club for an annual cattle show, and later used as a place of entertainment.

Crossing the road to the edge of what remains of the old village green we find the **statue of Sir Hugh Myddleton** (3), a sixteenth-century Welshman who founded a company that brought fresh spring water from Amwell, near Ware in Hertfordshire, to the City of London. The sculptor was John Thomas.

**Islington Green** (4) lies at the junction of Upper Street and Essex Road and was given to the parish by the lord of the manor. For many years it was a piece of unenclosed waste land used by the parishioners as a rubbish dump, but it was enclosed in 1777. In the centre stood the cage or prison and a pair of stocks. The green was also used as a place of assembly and after the passing of the Reform Act in 1832 the hustings and polling booth for the area were set up here.

On the far side of the Green was the famous **Collins music hall** (5), marked by a blue plaque. It opened in 1862 and closed in 1958. It was named after a chimney sweep, whose stage name was Sam Collins, and who converted a public house on the site into the music hall.

Further along Upper Street the **parish church of St Mary,** Islington (6), is soon reached. The Abbots of Westminster had a chapel here but it is not recorded when the first church was built. During the middle ages there was a shrine dedicated to 'Our Ladie of Iseldon', but this was swept away at the Reformation in the sixteenth century. Severely damaged in the Second World War, the church was rebuilt and re-dedicated in 1956; only the tower and spire remain of the eighteenth-century church designed by Launcelot Dowbiggin.

Centre of the administration of the borough of Islington is the **Town Hall** (7), designed by E. C. P. Morison and opened in 1925.

Our way leads past the **Union Chapel** (8), the leading nonconformist meeting place in the borough today. Built in 1876, to the designs of James Cubitt, it typifies the high Gothic style of the late nineteenth century.

Soon after the chapel Canonbury Lane is reached. Turn into the lane, which takes its name from the house (bury) of the

# ISLINGTON

1 The Angel
2 Royal Agricultural Hall
3 Statue of Sir Hugh Myddleton
4 Islington Green
5 Collins music hall
6 St Mary's church
7 Town Hall
8 Union Chapel
9 Canonbury Tower
10 Canonbury Place
11 Highbury Fields
12 Cross Street
13 Camden Passage
14 Duncan Terrace

Augustinian Canons of St Bartholomew the Great in Smithfield, just outside the City of London. It is not far to Canonbury Square, dominated by the remains of **Canonbury Tower** (9). The tower reminds us that in the thirteenth century Ralph de Berners gave the Manor of Islington to the Canons of St Bartholomew's. The tower itself was built in the early sixteenth century during the office of William Bolton, the last prior of the order in Smithfield. His rebus, a visual pun on his name, can still be seen on a nearby house. It is an arrow (bolt) piercing a barrel (a tun), so making the word 'bolt-tun'. After the dissolution of the monastery in 1539 the property had several owners until 1570, when Alderman Sir John Spencer, who is buried in St Helen's church, Bishopsgate, bought the house and grounds for £2,000. The following century the estate passed to the Compton family through marriage. Extensively restored in 1952, part of the site is now occupied by a small theatre.

Before leaving the vicinity of the tower take a walk around the square to look at the architecture, which is early nineteenth-century. Some of the area beyond the tower has been rebuilt in recent years, while other parts have benefited from the work of the conservationists (10).

Compton Road, another reminder of past lords of the manor, leads to St Paul's Road. Turn left at the junction and you soon reach Highbury station (Victoria Line and British Rail). The road to the right of the station leads to **Highbury Fields** (11). If property developers had not taken over much of the land here, there might well have been another large park to rank with Hyde, Regent's, and St James's parks. A certain Mr Lloyd tried, in vain, to raise the required sum, about £250,000, to buy the land and to turn it into a vast public park which would have been as large as Regent's Park and Hyde Park put together. Lloyd interested the Prince Consort and several members of the aristocracy in his scheme but in the end the builders won the day and left Highbury Fields only a 'poor shadow of its former glorious self' for us to enjoy in the twentieth century. But it makes a pleasant enough oasis in an area surrounded by houses of varying quality.

Having rested awhile in the Fields, leave by way of Baalbec Road and, following through Highbury Grove, cross St Paul's Road once more. Your route now follows St Mary's Grove, Alwyne Place and Alwyne Road to Canonbury Road. Here turn left and soon Essex Road station is reached. Turn right and soon Islington Green will come into sight once more, but first visit **Cross Street** (12) with its lovely Adam-style houses.

On reaching the Green continue past **Camden Passage** (13), where you may well be attracted to spend a little time, and probably quite a lot of money, browsing among the antique shops. Passing the Myddleton statue on your right, walk along the High Street until Duncan Street is reached. Here turn left and it will lead you into **Duncan Terrace,** where Charles Lamb lived for a short time (14). His house is marked with a blue plaque. The terrace consists of two rows of houses facing each other across a landscaped square, but in Lamb's day the New River ran between them. This now runs underground and the land above provides a resting place for the weary walker.

# 11. Kew

In most people's minds Kew is synonymous with gardens and the untold delights of exploring the glasshouses and hothouses of the Royal Botanical Gardens. However, the village has much more to offer than the gardens and a short stroll in the area will soon convince the person in search of places of architectural and

## KEW

1 Kew Bridge
2 Kew Green
3 Parish church
4 Ferry Lane
5 Herbarium
6 Main gates of Kew Gardens
7 Aroid House
8 Sundial

9 Kew Palace
10 Orangery
11 Lake
12 Queen's Cottage
13 Pagoda
14 Flagstaff
15 Palm House and Queen's Beasts
16 Cambridge Cottage

historical interest.

The exact origin of the place-name Kew is obscure although there have been a number of attempts to define it. One can trace, apart from its modern spelling, eight different forms in various documents. In the court roll of Richmond, at the time of Henry VII, it is written *Kayhough,* or *Keyho* during the reign of Henry VIII, while in later documents it is given variously as *Kayhowe, Kayhoo, Keyhowe, Keye, Kaiho,* and *Kewe.*

Linking Kew, on the south (Surrey) side of the river, with Brentford on the north (Middlesex) side were two ferries. One was a horse ferry which was owned in the eighteenth century by Robert Tunstall, and the other, lower, ferry was known as Powel's, or the foot ferry. In February 1757 Parliament was petitioned and an Act, with royal assent, was passed to provide a bridge across the Thames in June of the same year. The site chosen was where Tunstall's Ferry plied for hire across the river, but in December 1757 Parliament was again petitioned, this time with objections to the chosen site and with recommendations that the lower ferry site should be used. In 1758 the second Act was passed and, with the petitioners' success, the bridge was duly built on the second site. Robert Tunstall financed the project, no doubt with an eye to the future revenue from the tolls. The bridge was opened by the Prince of Wales, later George III, on 4th June 1759. It lasted until 1782, when Parliament was asked to sanction its rebuilding. The second bridge, built between 1783 and 1789, had a contract price of £11,864 and James Paine (c 1716-89) as architect. Meanwhile the old wooden bridge, slightly downstream from the new one, was repaired and kept in use until Paine's bridge was finished. In 1874 the bridge was declared 'free of toll', with a compensation fee of £57,000 being paid to the owners. In 1895 steps were taken to replace the bridge once more. The Kew Bridge Act of 1898 empowered the Surrey and Middlesex county councils to rebuild the bridge. Work began in 1899 and the present bridge was opened on 20th May 1903 by Edward VII. It was announced that it would be called the 'King Edward VII's Bridge', but it is still today known as **Kew Bridge** (1).

**Kew Green** (2), originally an open, unfenced space of some thirty acres, today occupies a slightly lesser area. It is certainly kept in better order now than in the eighteenth and nineteenth centuries when there are a number of complaints in the vestry minutes of rubbish being dumped on the green. Until they were abolished by the vestry in 1781, fairs were regularly held on the green, but because of the nuisance they caused the vestry acted to close them.

Opposite the west door of the **church** (3) is the porch of Cambridge Cottage, now a museum of the gardens (see below).

A private chapel at Kew in the house of Thomas and Anne Byrkis was licensed by Richard Fox, Bishop of Winchester, in 1522. This was not a parochial church or chapel but one for the private use of the Byrkis family, and there was a clause in the document reserving all rights to the Vicar of Kingston, in whose parish Kew was then situated. The chapel seems to have sufficed local needs until the beginning of the eighteenth century when, in 1710, application was made for a parochial church to be built on the green. Queen Anne took an interest in the project, presented the site and in addition gave £100 towards the building fund. Appropriately, or perhaps because of the royal patronage, the church was dedicated to Saint Anne, the mother of the Blessed Virgin Mary, and on 12th May 1714 was consecrated, with the Vicar of Kingston preaching the sermon. With the growth of population in the area, the original church, which had only twenty-one pews, became too small and had to be enlarged. By 1884 it had increased to 737 seats, of which two hundred were to be free - under a provision of William IV - and there is an inscription in the gallery to this effect. Pew rents were levied in the eighteenth and nineteenth centuries in a large number of churches and formed a useful part of the income of the parish.

In 1851 a mausoleum was added at the east end and later incorporated into the new (1884) chancel, for the remains of the Duke and Duchess of Cambridge. The building today is a chapel of rest for the ashes of parishioners, the Cambridge family remains having been removed to Windsor at the wish of Queen Mary, their granddaughter, whose parents, the Duke of Teck and the Duchess (nee Princess Mary of Cambridge) were married in the church.

The organ, a gift to the church by George IV, is said to have been the favourite instrument of George III and also of G. F. Handel (1685-1759), both of whom played it regularly.

Thomas Gainsborough (1727-88), one of the founders of the Royal Academy in 1768, was buried in the churchyard near the south wall of the church. Although he never lived in Kew he often visited a friend here and grew to like the place so much that he left instructions in his will asking to be buried here. After his death his executors carried out his wish. Near his grave is that of his friend Joshua Kirby (1716-74), the architect, whose works included additions to Kew church. He is better known, however, for his writings than for his buildings.

At the east end of the churchyard is the tomb of John Zoffany RA (1733-1810), a portrait painter of considerable reputation whose works can be seen in many galleries throughout Britain.

Along the north side of the green are a number of interesting eighteenth-century houses. Beside one of them runs **Ferry Lane** (4), its name reminding us of the ferries that used to ply between the Surrey and Middlesex banks of the river Thames. The short lane leads the explorer to the riverbank and, by turning left, to a pleasant walk along the riverside.

Although not open to the public, but only to *bona fide* students and qualified research workers, the **Herbarium** (5) is housed in a Georgian-style house, with later additions. It contains a splendid collection of dried plants, which forms an important department of the Royal Botanical Gardens. There are millions of samples from all over the world, which botanists from every country come to consult. The library contains some fifty to sixty thousand volumes and is the finest taxonomic library in Europe, if not in the whole world.

At the far end of the green are the **main gates to the Royal Botanical Gardens** of Kew (6). The gates and their side screens were designed by Decimus Burton (1800-81), the famous architect whose London buildings include the Athenaeum Club (1828-30) and the arch at the top of Constitution Hill, a memorial to the first Duke of Wellington (1825-6). The gates form a fitting end to the green and a magnificent entrance to the gardens.

**Kew Gardens** or, to give them their correct title, the Royal Botanical Gardens, Kew, are universally famous, cover some 270 acres and contain as wide a variety of plants as can be seen anywhere else in the world.

Owing their origin to the private gardens of Sir Henry Capsel, who died in 1696 and who in his travels in France collected many rare trees and fruits, they have since 1841 been open for the public to enjoy their beauty. John Evelyn (1620-1706) makes a number of references to the gardens in the seventeenth century, commenting at one point, on there being too many trees, but admiring the glasshouses for the oranges and myrtle.

During the eighteenth century Capability Brown (1715-83) landscaped the gardens and Sir William Chambers (1726-96), the architect, embellished the grounds with temples and other buildings.

First open to the public in 1841, the gardens were handed over to the state by Queen Victoria. They are a centre for scientific research projects that may have far-reaching effects all over the world. It was once estimated that if the gardens were closed to sightseers for a few years most of the world's food shortage problems could be solved by the scientists of Kew.

Leaving the main gates behind us, and, having consulted the map of the gardens and read the rules - a fascinating collection of official jargon - we walk ahead and discover the first of many interesting glasshouses in the grounds. The **Aroid House** (7), whose normal temperature is 80 degrees Fahrenheit, has an interesting history, having been initially built as part of Buckingham Palace. When John Nash (1752-1835), the Prince Regent's favourite architect, was commissioned to restore the palace, he almost rebuilt it. His design included the erection of four temple-like buildings. In an adaptation of the buildings by Edward Bloner this temple was removed and re-erected here in 1836. The house contains specimens of plants from humid tropical forests - the aroids. Because of its unusual origin the house is the oldest one of its kind in the gardens.

From the seventeenth-century sundial (8), erected in 1832 by William IV in the forecourt of **Kew Palace** (9), and which marks the site of the main building of the White House, it is a short walk across the lawn to the **Orangery** (10). It was built in 1761, to the design of Sir William Chambers, for the Princess of Wales, whose coat of arms is carved over the central pediment of the building. The princess, Augusta of Saxe-Gotha, had married in 1737 Frederick, Prince of Wales, who died in 1751, the son of George II. Their son was to become George III.

The Orangery is one of several buildings erected for the princess by the same architect. Others are the Pagoda (1761-2), the Temple of Bellona (War) (1760), the Temple of Arethusa and the Temple of Aeolus (1761). Although built to house oranges and other exotic plants, over the years it has·been used for a number of purposes, including that of museum, but today it houses an exhibition of basic information to show the visitor to Kew what is to be seen and how scientific work is carried out, in addition to a small collection of paintings.

To construct the artificial **lake** (11) an area of four and a half acres was excavated and a culvert, one hundred yards in length, was laid to connect the former gravel pit with the river Thames. The river is the only source of supply of water and the lake can be replenished only at high tide, and then usually only at the time of a new or full moon. Four islands of varying sizes add further to the selection of plants in the gardens by displaying, amongst other items, swamp cypress, *Taxodium distichum,* while the banks on the Boathouse Walk side have firs. On the opposite side of the lake is Syon Vista with its view of the river frontage of Syon House, former home of the Dukes of Northumberland, on the Middlesex bank of the river.

Although the gardens were handed over to the state in 1841 Queen Victoria retained the **Queen's Cottage** (12) until 1897. At that time she handed over the cottage and the thirty-seven acres of woodlands surrounding it to commemorate her Diamond Jubilee. She did, however, place a condition on the gift that they should be kept in their semi-wild state. The cottage, built in 1760 to a design by Queen Charlotte for George III and their family, was used by the royal family as a summerhouse, where picnics could be held, and later as a shooting box.

Finding one's way round Kew Gardens requires either a skill at map reading, for there are some fifteen miles of paths made from material excavated from the area now occupied by the lake, or the use of landmarks. One such prominent building is the **Pagoda** (13), which was erected in 1761-2 from the designs of Sir William Chambers, whose other works here have already been noted. Sir William's father was a Scottish merchant who was living in Stockholm at the time of his son's birth; shortly afterwards the family left Sweden and settled in Ripon, North Yorkshire. At the age of sixteen Chambers was sent to the East Indies and China as supercargo and with the intention of following his father's trade. He appears to have become fascinated by Chinese architecture and spent much of his time sketching. After leaving the service of the Swedish East India Company in 1749, he began his serious study of architecture and spent the rest of his life as an architect. It was to his early youth that he turned for inspiration for the Pagoda. It stands 163 feet high with ten storeys, the lowest level being 26 feet in diameter and 18 feet high, each succeeding storey decreasing by a foot in height and diameter. The building is made of stock brick and timber. The interior consists entirely of the central staircase which links the various floor levels. Although it was built in six months, its sturdiness was well put to the test in the Second World War, when a number of high explosive bombs fell nearby.

Soaring 225 feet into the sky, the **Flagstaff** (14), the fourth one to be erected in the gardens, was the gift of the people of British Columbia, presented to commemorate the centenary of the Canadian province (1958), and the bicentenary of the gardens (1959). The tree, a Douglas fir weighing thirty-nine tons, had a diameter, at the base, of over six feet, and was about 370 years old when it was cut down and before it was shaped. After shaping its weight was reduced to fifteen tons and the base to 2 feet 9 inches square, finally tapering to one foot at the tip.

Once the largest glasshouse of its kind in the world, the **Palm House** (15) was designed by Decimus Burton; erected between 1844 and 1848, it can be compared with his similar construction at Chatsworth House, Derbyshire (1836-40), demolished in 1920, though plans and drawings of it still exist. The Palm House is just over 120 yards in length and has a crossing (transept) 100 feet wide and 66 feet high, and two wings each of which are 50 feet wide and 30 feet high. It contains plants from the tropics of both hemispheres. The house gets its name from the wide variety of palms, or cycads, that can be seen there.

Lining the south side of the Palm House are the **Queen's Beasts.** Originally made of plaster and erected outside the specially constructed Coronation Annexe to Westminster Abbey, they were designed by James Woodford OBE, RA, and show the direct lineage of Her Majesty the Queen from Edward III (1312-77). These beasts are stone replicas of those used at the Coronation and are an anonymous gift to the gardens.

Already mentioned as having its front entrance overlooking the green, **Cambridge Cottage** (16), dating from the eighteenth century, today houses the Wood Museum of the gardens. Once the home of the Duke and Duchess of Cambridge, it became a museum in 1910, at first being used to show British forestry. Since 1957 its function has been changed to that of a general wood and timber museum with special emphasis on timber from the Commonwealth countries. There is also a very attractive walled garden within the grounds.

# 12. Paddington

'A village situated on the Edgware Road, about a mile from London'; this is how a writer described Paddington in 1814. It could hardly be described that way today, but there are still parts of what is now the City of Westminster that retain their village-like

## PADDINGTON

1 Saint Mary's Church, Paddington Green
2 Grave of Sarah Siddons
3 Grave of Robert Haydon
4 Site of Greville House
5 Statue of Sarah Siddons
6 Saint Mary's Hospital
7 Milestone
8 Norfolk Square gates
9 O'Meara's house
10 Cambridge Square
11 Burwood Place
12 Parish Church of Saint John and Saint Michael
13 Victoria public house
14 Former burial ground wall
15 Tyburn Convent
16 Tyburn Tree plaque

atmosphere. Here during Saxon times came the Paeda family, and they set up a homestead. The ending 'ton' denoted a farm or homestead; this added to the family name gives us the present name of Paddington. As in other villages, life centred around the parish church of Paddington, which until the nineteenth century was Saint Mary's, Paddington Green, but since 1845 Saint James's, Sussex Gardens, has been the prime church of the 'village'.

**Saint Mary's Church, Paddington Green** (1), is the third church on or near this site, the present building having being erected between 1788 and 1791 to the designs of John Plaw, architect. Built in the form of a Greek cross, it is often taken to be a Greek Orthodox church, particularly as there is a Greek inscription over the south doorway. It is the oldest building still standing in Paddington.

Buried in the crypt of the church, not open to the public, is Dr Barry Edward O'Meara, doctor-surgeon to Napoleon, in a grave described as being 'in the right vault under the church, right-hand avenue near the door'. However, this was all bricked over and concreted when the crypt was used as a shelter during the First World War.

In the north churchyard can be seen the **grave of Sarah Siddons,** the actress (2). Her first London appearance was in 1775 at the Drury Lane Theatre, playing Portia in Shakespeare's *Merchant of Venice,* and her last performance was as Lady Macbeth at Covent Garden Theatre. Her funeral on 15th June 1831 drew over five thousand people, members of the theatre as well as of her public following.

Also in the burial ground north of the church, but in unconsecrated earth, is the **grave of Robert Haydon** (3), the artist who in 1846 committed suicide in Burwood Place. Haydon spent the latter years of his life in Paddington painting enormous, unsalable paintings of religious and Shakespearian themes. His greatest disappointment was not being asked to design or paint the murals for the newly built Houses of Parliament, then the Royal Palace of Saint Stephen at Westminster.

On the north side of Paddington Green (4), where now the Paddington Technical College stands, was **Greville House.** Here Emma Hart, or Lyon, the later Lady Hamilton (*c* 1765-1815), was once employed as a servant.

A **statue of Sarah Siddons** (5), depicted as the Tragic Muse and modelled on a painting by Sir Joshua Reynolds, stands on Paddington Green. The first London statue to be erected of a lady other than a member of the royal family, it was unveiled by Sir Henry Irving.

In a small laboratory overlooking busy Praed Street Alexander Fleming, apparently quite by accident, discovered *Penicillium notatum.* By chance a mould spore blew in through an open window on to a culture dish and was dissolved by the contents of the dish. A plaque placed on the outer wall of **Saint Mary's Hospital** (6) records the event, as well as one, not viewable, inside the hospital.

On the corner of Star Street and Edgware Road (7), in the front window of Lloyds Bank can be seen an ancient **milestone** inscribed to the effect that Tyburn is half a mile away.

At the east end of **Norfolk Square** (8) there are bar-gates across the road which prevent vehicles from entering the square from Norfolk Place. In the early nineteenth century there was a reservoir here, but in 1848 All Saints Church, now demolished, was built on the site, to the design of H. Clutton.

Today **No. 32 Sussex Gardens** (9) is a hotel, but in the nineteenth century, when the house was No. 16 Cambridge Terrace (Sussex Gardens came into being in 1938 with the renaming of Oxford and Cambridge Terraces), it was here that Barry Edward O'Meara lived and died.

To Thomas Armitage and William Ewart **Cambridge Square** (10) today would be unrecognisable with all its modern buildings. But from 1866 to 1886 Thomas Armitage lived at what was then No. 33, from where he strongly advocated the use of the Braille system for reading by the blind. He was also the founder of the British and Foreign Blind Association, now the Royal National Institute for the Blind.

William Ewart (1798-1869) lived in the square between 1843 and his death. As a member of Parliament he was instrumental in the passing of the Act which abolished hanging in chains in 1834 and of that which in 1837 abolished capital punishment for cattle-stealing and similar offences. His attempts to get the complete abolition of capital punishment failed, although he did succeed in raising a select committee to look into the question. In 1850 he sponsored the first Public Libraries Act which brought about the national library system of today by allowing local authorities to buy books from the rates for free lending to members of the public.

**Burwood Place** (11) is where Robert Haydon committed suicide in 1846 (see above). There is no trace today of the house in which he lived.

The **Parish Church of Saint John the Evangelist with Saint Michael and All Angels** (the latter church was previously in Star Street but was bombed in the Second World War) in Hyde Park Crescent (12) was built in 1832 and replaced the former Connaught Chapel. It is the second oldest church in Paddington and is said to have been inspired by New College, Oxford. The architect, Charles Fowler, also built a number of market houses including the ones at Covent Garden and Exeter.

For the drinker who likes to drink in a Victorian atmosphere the **Victoria public house** (13) in Strathearn Place is the place to go. Built about 1835, it has in its Gaiety Bar upstairs all the furnishings from the former Gaiety Theatre, which once stood at the Aldwych. The downstairs restaurant, 'Our Mutual Friend', reminds us that Charles Dickens lived in the close vicinity for a few weeks in 1870 while he was working on his unfinished novel *Edwin Drood*.

An area that is shown on the maps of the eighteenth century as a place of execution for soldiers and which later became the **burial ground** for the parishioners of Saint George's Church, Hanover Square, today has flats built on it (14). The burial ground was created in 1763, covering one acre, and it was used until it became full in 1852. Later it was used as a garden and the Royal Toxophilitic Society set up its butts in a cleared portion. Laurence Sterne, author of *Tristram Shandy* and *A sentimental journey,* was buried here in 1768; after his burial body-snatchers removed his corpse from its grave and sold it to the professor of anatomy at Cambridge, who on seeing his late friend's body returned it immediately to London. Doubt had been sown in some people's minds as to whether or not the body had been returned to the grave, but when the area was cleared before the building of the flats all the remains of the burials were removed. Particular care was taken over the grave of Sterne and a careful examination found the body - and two heads, one of which was verified as belonging to Sterne. The completed skeleton was then reinterred in Coxwold, the tiny Yorkshire village of which he was rector.

The artist Paul Sandby, who died in 1809, was also buried here. Born in 1721 at Nottingham, he is reputed to have introduced the aquatint into England from France; certainly he and his brother Thomas used this technique. Paul produced a series of etchings of Hyde Park and a number of his prints are in the Royal Library at Windsor where his brother was Deputy Ranger of Windsor Forest. In order to prevent any further body-snatching from the graveyard, two six-foot walls, three feet apart, were erected. Supposedly it is not possible to throw a corpse up and over such a wall.

Beside the **Tyburn Convent** (15) is the smallest house in London. Only three feet six inches wide, it was built to block a passage which the owner wanted to make private. The convent itself houses a Catholic religious order of nuns who, following the rule of Saint Benedict, dedicate their lives to the Sacred Heart by the perpetual adoration of the Blessed Sacrament. Founded in France in the last century, they were driven by the persecution of their order in 1901 from their home on Montmartre - the Mount of Martyrs - and settled here near the Hill of Martyrs - Tyburn, with its fateful gallows. In the crypt chapel there are many relics of saints who have died for their faith and at set times during the day it is possible to visit the chapel and to hear about the martyrs.

On a triangular road island opposite the Odeon Theatre, Edgware Road, is a plaque commemorating the site of **Tyburn Tree** (16). The tree, last used in 1783 for the hanging of John

Austin, stood twelve feet high, was triangular in shape and was capable of hanging eight people on each of its three sides. It was not unusual for gallows and other places of execution to be sited at the entrance to towns as a warning to potential criminals. This tree was the place of execution for felons from Newgate Prison, as well as for the martyrs of the Catholic Church for whom the nuns perpetually pray at their convent.

---

# 13. Stoke Newington

The interpretation of the name Stoke Newington reveals that it dates from Saxon times and means a new town (*ton*) in or near to a wood, but as a clearing in the wood the place can claim an origin in prehistoric times. With the setting up of the new London boroughs in the 1960s Stoke Newington became part of the London Borough of Hackney, from which it had been separated since the end of the last century.

In medieval times social life centred round the parish church and manor house; Ermine Street, the Roman road that runs along the boundary, brought visitors passing through on their travels to or from the City of London. By the sixteenth century Stoke Newington had acquired some importance, but little remains of this period. Some large houses of the seventeenth and eighteenth centuries can, however, still be seen.

Built on the site of a row of Georgian houses the 'new' **Town Hall** of Stoke Newington (1) was opened in 1937. Although no longer the centre of local government, it still serves the local community in other ways. It is a pleasant building, typical of the inter-war period. From its forecourt one can observe the two parish churches of the village.

Next to the Town Hall, with the Reference Library built on to it, is the **Central Lending Library** (2), erected in 1892, only two years after the Vestry adopted the Public Libraries Act. In the entrance hall is the memorial to local men killed in the First World War and there is an exhibition hall used for local prints and a collection of paintings. On permanent display in the hall is a very fine bust of Daniel Defoe, who lived in the parish during the early eighteenth century, and there is a commemorative plaque to Edgar Allan Poe, who attended the Manor House School.

The corner of Church Street and Edwards Lane was the site of the Manor House School, and Poe's association with it is marked by a blue plaque (3). Poe stayed in England between 1815 and 1820. His headmaster, Dr Dransby, was also the pastor of the local church and Poe describes his ascent into the pulpit on a Sunday morning in *William Wilson*. The headmaster said that Poe, 'who went under the name of Allan', was 'likable', but 'his parents spoilt him by allowing him too much pocket money. He was intelligent, wayward and wilful.'

**Stoke Newington Church Street** (4) contains an interesting selection of domestic architecture from the seventeenth to twentieth centuries. The elegant houses that face the end of Edwards Lane are typical of the early seventeenth century: red brick, white sash windows, a doorway to the hall and the front room of the ground floor in which to receive guests, with a simple ironwork railing.

A house on the corner of Defoe Road is marked with a blue plaque recording that Daniel Defoe lived here (5). The actual house in which he lived was demolished in 1865, when the present one was built, and is described as being 'gloomy and of irregular bricks'. Here Defoe wrote his most famous book, *Robinson Crusoe*, which was first published in 1719, two years after he moved to Stoke Newington. He also wrote here one of his pamphlets that led to his being fined, pilloried and imprisoned — *The Shortest Way with Dissenters;* later came *Moll Flanders* and *A Journal of the Plague Year*.

Shortly after leaving the site of Defoe's house, but on the same side of the road, there is a short terrace of houses dating from the late seventeenth or early eighteenth century (6). Notice in particular the overmantels of the doorways, which are charming examples of the period. Nearby, set back from the present footpath, is another pair of houses from the eighteenth century.

The only reminders of the former house and grounds of **Abney Park** (7) are the entrance gateway and some wrought iron railings. Built at the end of the seventeenth century, the house was handsome and convenient. It was later used as a training college for Wesleyans. Much of the grounds was turned into the Abney Park Cemetery in the nineteenth century.

The name of **Fleetwood Street** (8) commemorates the large and handsome house that once stood here, occupied by a distinguished Cromwellian soldier, Colonel Fleetwood. At the Restoration of the Monarchy in 1660 he was fortunate in receiving no punishment other than being 'perpetually incapacitated from all offices of trust', even though he had married Bridget, the widow of General Ireton and daughter of Oliver Cromwell. The house was of a mixture of styles from Jacobean to Palladian and was demolished in 1872. The materials from the mansion were used to build the houses on the site of its gardens. Parts of the finely carved ceiling are preserved at the public library.

One of the most unusual burials of all time took place in Stoke Newington in 1764: a local Quaker by the name of John Wilmer lived in fear of being buried alive and left specific instructions in his will that he should be buried in a bed with a table and chair by the side of it in case he awoke from his 'sleep'. In addition a wire

## STOKE NEWINGTON

1 Town Hall
2 Central Lending Library
3 Site of Manor House School
4 Houses opposite Edwards Lane
5 Site of Daniel Defoe's house
6 Houses of c. 1700
7 Abney Park
8 Fleetwood Street
9 Whincop's timber yard
10 The Three Crowns
11 No. 187 Stoke Newington High Street
12 Abney Park Cemetery
13 Presbyterian church
14 New River
15 Clissold Park
16 Parish church of St Mary
17 New St Mary's church
18 Newington Green

was to be attached to his wrist and connected to a bell in the coachman's house. But the family waited in vain for the summons. The wire rusted and was cut off from the bell, and the garden was built over, although many say that he still lies there on his bed waiting to wake up. Part of the site of his house and garden is now occupied by **Whincop's timber yard** (9).

Shortly after the timber yard Stoke Newington Church Street joins Stoke Newington High Street and on the corner stands the **Three Crowns** public house (10). It was so named after the three crowns of England, Scotland and Ireland to mark the progress through the area of James I of England (James VI of Scotland) when he came to claim the throne of England on the death of Elizabeth I in 1603.

Leaving the Three Crowns tavern, turn left and soon on the same side of the road are two interesting eighteenth-century houses. **No. 187** (11), in need of restoration, is shown on earlier maps as Halfway House but something of its former splendour can still be seen through the padlocked gates. Its neighbour is still in use as offices, but No. 191 no longer serves its former purpose as a hostel for fallen women.

The entrance to **Abney Park Cemetery** (12) looks like the forecourt of an Egyptian temple. But the cemetery, in the grounds of the former Abney Park House, has suffered from neglect over the past few years. However, it is well worth making a short exploration of it. Here are buried General Booth, the founder of the Salvation Army, and his wife, while under the church Bridget Fleetwood, Oliver Cromwell's daughter, was buried. There is also a life-size memorial by the sculptor E. H. Bailey to Isaac Watts, who lived at one time in Fleetwood House, but he is actually buried in Bunhill Fields. The architect of the cemetery, opened in 1840, was William Hoskings, later Professor of Architecture and Engineering Construction at King's College, London.

Returning to the entrance of the cemetery, turn left and walk up towards Stamford Hill. When Manor Road is reached turn left once again and walk along to the **Presbyterian church** (13), on the corner of Lordship Road. Turn right up Lordship Road and about a quarter of a mile along there is a tiny bridge over some water. This is the **New River** (14), engineered in the early seventeenth century by Hugh Myddleton, bringing fresh water from Ware in Hertfordshire to Stoke Newington. Originally the open channels continued to Roseberry Avenue, near the Sadlers Wells Theatre. Today the water is fed into the huge reservoirs here and, after filtering in the nearby Green Lanes waterworks pumping station, is piped to the taps of the Metropolis. The old pumping house seen on the skyline dates from 1854. It was designed by Chadwell Mylne to look like a medieval castle because the local inhabitants had objected to the erection of the pumping station on the grounds that it would spoil the view from their houses.

After admiring the view, and perhaps passing judgement on the nearby Woodberry Down Comprehensive School, retrace your steps to Manor Road. Then turn right along Lordship Park until Queen Elizabeth's Walk is reached. Turn left along the Walk to **Clissold Park** (15), which covers 54 acres (22 hectares). It takes its name from the Reverend Augustus Clissold who was curate at the parish church. He married one of the daughters of Mrs Crawshay, the owner of the house and grounds, and so came into possession of them. Later the property was put up for sale and two local residents, John Runtz and Joseph Beck, brought about its purchase as a public park for £96,000. The two benefactors are commemorated on a granite fountain in the centre of the park. The park contains a small zoo, with wallabies and rabbits. The former residence, built in 1790, is now used as a refreshment place. Tennis courts, a children's playground, a bowling green and a bandstand are other facilities. The lakes here were once claypits, dug to make bricks for the house, and now are the home of waterfowl. The New River also flows through part of the park and gulls in the winter swoop over the heads of strollers.

After visiting the park look for the twin spires of the old and new parish churches. When Stoke Newington was a small village the spiritual needs of the parish were well cared for by the small **parish church of St Mary's** (16). Originally built in the middle ages, the present church was 'newly rebuilt' in 1563 by the Lord of the Manor, William Patten, whose coat of arms is over the south-east doorway. Inside there is a memorial to John Dudley, whose widow, Elizabeth, married Thomas Sutton, the founder of the Charterhouse in the City.

A new church designed by Sir Gilbert Scott in the Decorated style of the middle ages was consecrated in 1858; the spire was added later by his son, John Oldrid Scott. The church is a noble building without and within, and it has been suggested that should the Diocese of London ever be split up this church could become the cathedral of North London. **New St Mary's** (17) has a number of interesting memorials, including one to the Rev. Thomas Jackson, vicar of the parish from 1852 to 1886, during which time the transfer from the old to the new church took place. Both churches were bombed in the Second World War, and the congregation worshipped in the old church until the new one was completely restored in the 1950s.

Now walk from the Town Hall down Albion Road to **Newington Green** (18); although not strictly in the parish of Stoke Newington it is a rewarding place at which to finish. The Unitarian Chapel was built in 1708, when this area was being settled by non-conformists, who had been ejected from the Church of England under the Act of Uniformity of 1662. In addition to chapels academies of education for their ministers and lay preachers were firmly established here. Mary Wollstonecraft rented a house on the Green and opened up a school for twenty pupils; her pamphlets on education and the rights of women brought her in touch with some of the leading thinkers of her time. She married William Godwin and their daughter, Mary, who married Shelley the poet, wrote the novel *Frankenstein*. As late as 1859 the Green is described as being of a rural nature; today the Green remains but rural England has moved away.

# Index

Abney Park 60, 62
Albert Bridge 48
Angel 46
Archway 45
Arnold, Benedict 6
Bacon, Francis 41
Barry, Sir Charles 19
Battersea 3-7
Bazalgette, Sir Joseph 4, 7, 23, 30
Bentley, John 17, 29
Blake, William 4-5
Blood, Thomas 6
Booth, General 62
Broomhouse Dock 24
Brown, Capability 52
Bulwer-Lytton, Sir Edward 21
Burlington, Earl of 15
Butterwick 29
Camden Passage 48
Canonbury Tower 47
Carlyle, Thomas 10
Chambers, Sir William 52, 53
Charles II 6, 7, 44
Chelsea 7-12
Chelsea Bridge 4
Cheyne Walk 8, 9
Chichester, Sir Francis 25
Chiswick 12-15
Clapham 16-19
Clissold Park 62
Coleridge, Samuel 39
Constable, John 34, 37
Cook, Captain 19
Craven Cottage 21
Crosby Hall 9
Curtis, William 6
Cutty Sark 26
Danvers, Sir John 9
Defoe, Daniel 59, 60
Dickens, Charles 28, 37, 38, 58
Doggett's Coat and Badge 8
Dwight, John 20
Edward VII 15, 23
Eliot, George 7, 43
Evelyn, John 19, 22, 32, 52
Faraday, Michael 43
Fenton House 36
Flamsteed, John 27
Fleming, Alexander 56
Flitcroft, Henry 36
Foscolo, Ugo 14

Friese-Green, William 43
Fulham 19-24
Gainsborough, Thomas 51
Gaitskell, Hugh 34
Galsworthy, John 37
Gaskell, Mrs 9
Gibbons, Grinling 19, 25
Gipsy Moth IV 25
Gladstone, William 28
Greenwich 24-9
Gwynne, Nell 44
Hamilton, Emma 56
Hammersmith 29-33
Hampstead 33-8
Handel, G. F. 51
Hawksmoor, Nicholas 24, 26
Haydon, Robert 56, 57
Henry VIII 8, 10, 24, 27
Highbury Fields 48
Highgate 38-45
Hill, Sir Rowland 43
Hogarth, William 12, 13-14, 42
Hood, Thomas 19
Hunt, Leigh 11, 36, 37
Hurlingham 23
Isle of Dogs 25
Islington 45-8
Jack Straw's Castle 37
Jones, Inigo 14, 26
Keats, John 37
Kelmscott House 31
Kent, William 15
Kew 48-54
Lamb, Charles 36, 48
Lauderdale House 44
Linden House 32
Lindsay House 10
Lloyd George 8
Louterbourg, Philip de 32
Macaulay, Lord 17
Marvell, Andrew 44
Marx, Karl 43
More, Thomas 8, 9, 10
Morris, William 31, 32
Myddleton, Sir Hugh 46, 62
National Army Museum 11
National Maritime Museum 27, 28
Newington Green 63
New River 62
O'Meara, Barry 56, 57

Paddington 54-9
Paxton, Joseph 14
Pepys, Samuel 18, 19, 44
Poe, Edgar Allan 59
Putney 23
Queen's Beasts 54
Queen's House 26
Ravenscourt Park 33
Rogers, Robert 42
Romney, George 36
Rossetti, Dante G. 8
Royal Hospital 7, 11
Royal Naval College 26
Royal Observatory 27
St Mary's Hospital 56
St Paul's School 31
Sandby, Paul 58
Scott, George Gilbert 37
Scott, Robert 11
Scott, Walter 36
Siddons, Sarah 56
Spaniards Inn 38
Sterne, Laurence 58
Stoke Newington 59-63
Swinburne, Algernon 8
Tallis, Thomas 25
Thornhill, Sir James 26
Trinity Hospital 28
Turner, J. M. W. 6
Turpin, Dick 38, 42
Tyburn 58
University Boat Race 22, 30
Vale of Health 37
Vanbrugh, Sir John 26, 28
Walker, Sir Emery 32
Watermans Arms 25
Waterlow Park 43
Wellington, Duke of 4
Whistler, J. M. 8, 11, 14
Whitestone Pond 37
Whittington, Dick 45
Widanhurst 40
Wilberforce, William 5, 18
Wilde, Oscar 11
Wilson, Edward 6
Wolfe, James 25, 27
Wollstonecraft, Mary 63
Wren, Christopher 6, 19, 26, 29
Wyatt, James 15
Zinzendorf, Count 10
Zoffany, John 51